Sexing the Soldier

The politics of gender and the contemporary British Army

Rachel Woodward
and Trish Winter

LONDON AND NEW YORK

First published 2007
by Routledge
2 Park Square, Milton Park, Abingdon, Oxon OX14 5RN

Simultaneously published in the USA and Canada
by Routledge
270 Madison Ave, New York, NY 10016

Routledge is an imprint of the Taylor & Francis Group, an informa business

Typeset in Times New Roman by Prepress Projects, Perth, UK
Printed and bound in Great Britain by The Cromwell Press, Trowbridge, Wiltshire

British Library Cataloguing in Publication Data
A catalogue record for this book is available from the British Library

Library of Congress Cataloging in Publication Data
Woodward, Rachel.
Sexing the soldier : the politics of gender and the contemporary British Army / Rachel Woodward and Trish Winter.
p. cm.
1. Great Britain. Army – Women. 2. Women and the military – Great Britain. I. Winter, Trish. II. Title.
UB419.G7W66 2007
355.0082'0941 – dc22

ISBN 10: 0-415-39256-X (hbk)
ISBN 10: 0-415-39255-1 (pbk)
ISBN 10: 0-203-94625-1 (ebk)

ISBN 13: 978-0-415-39256-3 (hbk)
ISBN 13: 978-0-415-39255-6 (pbk)
ISBN 13: 978-0-203-94625-1 (ebk)

Contents

Acknowledgements

We would like to thank our colleagues at our respective universities for support during the research leading up to the production of this book, and for periods of research leave during which this book was written. Rachel Woodward would like to thank her colleagues at the Centre for Rural Economy, the Centre for Gender and Women's Studies, the School of Agriculture, Food and Rural Development, and the School of Geography, Politics and Sociology, all at Newcastle University. Rachel would also like to acknowledge the assistance given by the Defence Studies Forum at the Australian Defence Force Academy, who provided a base during study leave in 2004–5, to thank her hosts for their hospitality and to thank the staff at the ADFA Library for helping with access to their wonderful collections and facilities. Trish Winter would like to thank her colleagues in the School of Arts, Design, Media and Culture, and the Centre for Research in Media and Cultural Studies, both at the University of Sunderland.

We would like to acknowledge the support of the Economic and Social Research Council in funding some of the research on which this book is based, a project entitled 'Gendered bodies, personnel policies and the culture of the British Army', ESRC Reference R000223562. Funding through the Newcastle University Faculty of Science, Agriculture and Engineering Small Grants Scheme made other discrete pieces of research possible, which have also fed into the thinking behind this book.

We would also like to acknowledge how our thinking around these issues has benefited from a number of conversations over the years with our academic colleagues from the military studies community, in particular Victoria Basham, Tim Edmunds, Anthony Forster, Joan Heggie, Paul Higate, Neil Jenkings and Ann Murphy. We would also like to thank those members of the Ministry of Defence and the British Army who have shared their knowledge and opinions with us, both formally and off the record.

Finally, we would like to thank our respective families and friends for their love, support and good humour during the time we have spent researching and writing this book, especially Ged Lawson and Joe, Ruth and Patrick Painter.

Abbreviations

ADFA	Australian Defence Force Academy
AFOPS	Armed Forces Overarching Personnel Strategy
ALI	Adult Learning Inspectorate
ANC	African National Congress
ATR(W)	Army Training Regiment (Winchester)
ATRA	Army Training and Recruiting Agency
ATS	Auxiliary Territorial Services
AWOL	Absent Without Leave
BBC	British Broadcasting Corporation
CMS(R)	Common Military Syllabus (Recruits)
CO	Commanding Officer
CRE	Commission for Racial Equality
CSM	Company Sergeant Major
DASA	Defence Analytical Services Agency
EO	Equal Opportunities
EOC	Equal Opportunities Commission
ESRC	Economic and Social Research Council
EU	European Union
FANY	First Aid Nursing Yeomanry
HQ	Headquarters
HR	Human Resources
IDF	Israeli Defence Force
IRA	Irish Republican Army
IT	Information Technology
ITD(A)	Individual Training Directive (Army)
JEDTC	Joint Equality and Diversity Training Centre
MATT	Military Annual Training Test
MoD	Ministry of Defence
NATO	North Atlantic Treaty Organisation
NBC	Nuclear Biological Chemical
PE	Physical Education
PR	Public Relations

PSS(R)	Physical Selection Standards (Recruits)
RA	Royal Artillery
RAF	Royal Air Force
RE	Royal Engineers
REME	Royal Electrical and Mechanical Engineers
SADF	South African Defence Force
SANDF	South African National Defence Force
SAS	Special Air Service
TSEOTC	Tri-Service Equal Opportunities Training Centre
UN	United Nations
VAD	Voluntary Aid Detachment
WAAC	Women's Auxiliary Army Corps
WRAC	Women's Royal Army Corps

1 Gender and the British Army

Military, civilian and conceptual issues

This book is about the politics of gender and the British Army. The intention of this book is straightforward. We engage with a range of debates and arguments around men and women's participation in armed forces, we look in detail at one example from one place and time (the British Army, in the UK, at the beginning of the twenty-first century) and we ask two questions. The first question is: how does gender work as an axis of organisation within the contemporary British Army and what understandings of gender follow from this? The second question is: how does this military understanding of gender relate to civilian understanding of and responses to the British Army, the armed forces more widely, and military activities and militarism in general? In this book, we argue for a broader understanding and awareness of gender issues than that suggested by much contemporary military and public debate, with its focus on questions around women's military participation. We take the analysis of gender issues to include the study of both men and women. We are interested in the ways that gender difference, gender relations and gender identities shape military practices, and in the politics around the cultural practices that produce and reproduce ideas about gender as they circulate both around the Army and in wider contemporary civilian cultures and cultural forms.

Let us clarify at the outset our definitions of 'gender' and 'military', because our use of these two terms defines our field of study. We use the term 'gender' to refer to the structuring of social relations and individual identities around biological sex differences. People are born male or female, and usually remain so. Morphological or physiological differences between males and females are external manifestations of biological differences that have evolved for the reproduction of the human species. These biological reproductive differences denote sex. We are not, however, just biological beings; we are people, and people function as social beings. We use the term 'gender' to refer to the multiple and diverse ways in which social relations (how we relate to each other) and identity (what we feel ourselves to be) are formed and sustained around sex differences. Gender, then, is a social category based around sex differences.[1]

The term 'military', which we use interchangeably with 'armed forces', refers to the institutions and people working within those institutions that are granted licence by the state to exercise coercive force or violence.[2] This definition follows a Weberian tradition in Anglophone sociology and political science which understands the state as the institution, which holds the monopoly over the use of violence; the state confers the right to deploy that armed force, primarily to its military, for the pursuit its political objectives.[3] We focus here exclusively on the military and armed forces as institutions of the state, and do not include in our analysis gender issues within paramilitary and other non-state actors,[4] or broader issues about gender positions and experiences amongst civilian or non-combatant populations in war and armed conflict.[5]

Underpinning our whole argument about gender politics and the military is an observation about the contingency of military structure, culture and organisation. Armed forces, in order to deliver potentially lethal force in support of the political objectives of the state, are organised in specific and intentional ways. These modes of organisation, most obvious in the hierarchical structures and chains of command of the military, are manifest across the range of military functions, from divisions of labour to the use of weaponry, from the supply of matériel to the maintenance of a standing army. Everything that armed forces do is focused on developing and maintaining the capacity to deliver potentially lethal force. Organisational structures and operational cultures evolve and develop with that end in mind. What we want to make clear, right from the start, is that these structures and cultures are social in origin, devised by people, put into practice by people, changed by people. Military modes of organisation and the military cultures that support them are contingent and negotiated, and not essential and fundamental; there is nothing 'natural' or automatic in the gender politics of a military force.

Two further observations follow from this. The first is that, because armed forces are social organisations, they have to be examined with explicit reference to the sociocultural contexts within which they originate. Because they are instruments of the nation state, they cannot be understood without reference to the ideas and arguments through which the nation state is constituted and sustained. This observation has methodological and analytic consequences for the approach taken in this book. Although our arguments are framed with reference to often quite international academic and political debates about the gender politics of armed forces, our focus here is exclusively on the British case. There are a couple of reasons for this. One is that, as British academics working in and on the military and culture in the UK, the British case and context is the one we know and can speak with reasonable authority about. The other is that in the literatures on gender and the military, and the wider literatures on men, women and war, there are relatively few up-to-date accounts of the contemporary British Armed Forces. We can contrast the wealth of historical research on the British military experience with regard to gender with the dearth of critical scholarly analysis of this with regard to the British present.[6]

The organisational structures and gender cultures of military forces are specific to geographical space and historical period. There may well be historical parallels and similarities between different national armed forces, but those parallels and continuities need to be understood as contingent and circumstantial rather than absolute and transcendent of time and space. Although broad-brush trans-historical and cross-cultural studies of gender and the military are valuable for the methodological questions they raise and the wider conceptual lessons that we can learn from them,[7] more focused studies such as this are also necessary if we really want to get to grips with how gender works within military organisations and how gender politics affects how wider civil society understands military organisations. The wider applicability of focused studies derives from their method and analytic approach, rather than from any automatic universality in research findings.

Our second observation is about putting gender in its place. The structures and cultures of military organisations are contingent on the social practices, moral frameworks and cultural conventions that shape the people that put them into place, into operation, and into effect. Gender – whether in terms of difference, relation or identity – is just one part of the mixture of social practices that shape the organisational structures and operational cultures which, in turn, facilitate armed forces' abilities to deliver lethal force at the behest of the state. Gender is by no means the only part of the mix. In the British Armed Forces, for example, socioeconomic class, national and regional identification and ethnicity are extremely important too in structuring military identities and social relations within the forces. But gender is a significant part of the mix; we argue in this book that institutional structures, social relations, organisational cultures and operational modes are all gendered in some way. In writing a book solely about gender, we are not ultimately trying to privilege gender relative to other forms of social difference, but rather trying to draw conclusions about one specific aspect of social relations.[8] Gender fundamentally shapes and influences military practice, whether discursively through the conflation of specific forms of masculinity with military identity, materially through gender divisions of labour in different arms and services within the armed forces or geographically through the dynamics of shared and separate spaces and places for male and female military personnel. Gender in the military is an issue that is often obvious, apparent and visible. Equally, gender issues are frequently obscured, normalised, lived with and ignored. The one thing gender is not is ephemeral, whether to the British Army and armed forces or to the militaries of states around the world. In the next three sections, we explain why this is so; indeed, our rationale for writing this book springs from the following observations.

Gender is a military issue

Gender is an issue for all armed forces, in all sorts of ways, and a first rationale for this book is to argue for an understanding of gender in the armed forces as much more than questions around the sex of a minority of its personnel. Gender informs what contemporary militaries do, how they operate, how they are structured, how they are managed, how they understand themselves, how they and their roles are perceived by civil society and by the state. Gender is influential across such a range of military ideas and practices, shapes such a range of issues conceptually and materially, that arguably gender is everywhere in the military, as a factor influencing practice and as a feature of military practices. This in itself is unremarkable; armed forces are social entities, and militaries consequently share with all other social institutions their susceptibility to the influence of gender across the whole range of their actions, functions and organisation. Gender is an issue whether an armed force or units within that force are single-sexed or they are mixed. Gender is an issue, whether working relations within a unit of men and women are understood to be unproblematic (if so, what is it that makes them work that way?) or such relations are fraught and difficult (if so, why?). Gender informs the stories that circulate within an armed force which construct and reproduce its (dominantly masculine) identity, and the stories that circulate about an armed force within civilian culture and social life that interprets the military through a gendered lens. Gender, in short, is one of the frameworks through which military life is structured; gender is a military issue.

Gender is a military issue because it influences who will participate in a military force and who will not. In armed forces that select volunteers and in those that conscript a section of their host population, assumptions about the gendered nature of military formations shapes who is seen as a possible recruit and who is not. At a very crude level, we can see this in the division of the recruit pool according to sex. But the influence of gender goes way beyond this. Imagine a potential recruit undergoing a process of selection for any branch of any armed force. Gender is a factor influencing not only the judgements made about the physical capabilities (or otherwise) of that would-be recruit, but also the judgements made about the potential of that individual to develop appropriate abilities through the process of military training. Following selection, ideas about gender and its significance as a marker of difference shape how those recruits are trained and assumptions about what that training might possibly achieve for those recruits. The processes through which individual identities are reconfigured as military identities, through which people become soldiers (or the equivalent in naval and air forces), are processes that draw on norms and values which themselves are imbued with ideas about what is appropriate male and female behaviour, what is appropriate for men and women to do and what is appropriate for the ways in which men and women might relate to each other. Although the underlying norms and values governing gender identities and relations will differ markedly between armed forces, reflecting cultural differences within host societies, the inculcation of specific gender norms in the bodies and minds of military personnel is a process shared by all armed forces.

Gender is a military issue because it is an operational issue for military personnel. Gender politics will be at work in the uniforms that personnel wear, the ergonomics factored into the design of weapons and weapons systems, the operational division of labour in the use of weapons systems, and the organisational systems that maintain a fighting force capable of using those weapons systems. Gender relations and gender identities must be managed to build an operationally competent team, to develop a team that is sufficiently cohesive for efficacy, but not so self-referential as to limit its capabilities or produce adverse military effects. This applies whatever the sex distribution in an operational team, from single sex to equally mixed. Gender is a factor determining what men and women are permitted or forbidden to do, with themselves, with their own kind and with each other, but it also works more subtly in the absence of direct prohibition. Gender shapes how military personnel relate to one another, the development of workplace practices and what is determined as acceptable and unacceptable behaviour in the context of military operations and daily working life.

Gender is a military issue because the identities of different branches of armed forces, and of different arms and services within an armed force, are informed by ideas about gender roles. Gender is implicated not only in the divisions of labour between different operational units, but also in the very ways those units define themselves. Gender appears in the official public face of units, in quasi-official presentations (websites, for example) and in the more private practices through which units define who they are and what they are to themselves. The logics and practices of initiation rituals, for example, are saturated within gender politics. Processes of identity formation, whether public or private or somewhere in between, are practices in which gender is complicit.

Gender is a military issue because it shapes the practices of military living and the spaces in which that living takes place. It informs the understanding of the planners of military bases and barracks about who can and cannot live together, how they can live together, what facilities it is appropriate to share or not share, and how these spaces should visibly reflect their military function. Gender is there in the understanding of the users of military spaces, from the ways in which personal living and working spaces are decorated and individualised to the norms and modes of behaviour that determine how shared living and working spaces are used.

Gender is a military issue because military personnel are still people, enjoying private lives and loves and friendships. Gender shapes conventions around family roles and responsibilities, around care-giving and around responsibilities towards dependents. It informs the conduct of sexual relationships, partnerships and marriages involving military personnel. It informs assumptions about the provision of family accommodation and the provision of educational, health and welfare services to military dependents. It informs assumptions about the roles and positions of military spouses, whether on base or off site.

Gender issues are military issues because, in ways that are more cultural than material, ideas about gender are implicated in how the national purposes of an armed force are imagined. The values and ideologies that give meaning to military service in the minds of military personnel are shaped by ideas about men's and women's position relative to the nation state, just as civil society's imagination of the role of armed forces with respect to the nation state is influenced by gendered ideologies. For example, the maintenance of the state of Israel, forged and sustained through the exercise of military power, is supported by discourses around the rights and duties of its male (and sometimes female) citizens as military conscripts, which in turn are differentiated by ideologies around gender roles and the nation. In the US, discourses of citizenship and national service are deployed to give meaning to that service, seen increasingly in terms of the equity of duty.

In the UK, discourses explaining military participation as service to Queen and country may be dismissed in favour of ideas around service to the bonded team, an idea that relies for its force and coherence on ideas about military identity, which are gendered in construction and articulation.

Gender, then, is a military issue of some significance, and one which, in implication and consequence, goes way beyond questions about the sex distributions of its personnel. A first motivation for this book is therefore to map out some of the many ways in which gender politics play out in the British Army. We focus exclusively on the British Army, of the three armed services, with the expectation that some of our observations are applicable to the naval service and Royal Air Force, but mindful of the limits to applicability given the distinctive roles and functions of the three armed forces. Why the Army? Because, when we started research in this area, we were aware that, of the three armed forces in the UK, the Army had the highest proportion of men, the lowest proportion of women and the highest percentage of posts that were restricted to one sex and closed to the other, and seemed to face the greatest challenges in the integration of women, an issue explained through its function in deploying mobile, land-based units.[9]

Military gender issues are civilian issues

There are those who would see the business of armed forces, whether in terms of its gender politics or in terms of anything else, as the legitimate concern only of the armed forces. The 'armchair general' epithet is a common rebuke to those outside the military who offer comment on the internal workings of that military. This is an attitude that we reject. Gender issues, whether revolving around gender relations, or the construction and maintenance of gender identities, or conceptualised around the politics of gender difference, are significant issues for armed forces and their personnel, as we have already argued. But they are also profoundly and fundamentally important issues for civil society too, and so are legitimate areas for public debate. There are two principal reasons why this is so.

The first reason why military gender issues are civilian issues is the public interest argument. In the case of the British Army, as with the three armed forces and as with any military force that is funded through general taxation and answerable to a democratically elected government, we would argue for the need for public accountability about the internal operations of that armed force. As General Sir Rupert Smith has noted, we live in an age of growing public lack of interest in all aspects of military force.[10] Leaving aside the issue of secrecy for reasons of operational efficacy,[11] it is politically necessary in a healthy democracy for the activities of its armed forces to come under external public scrutiny. In Britain, that scrutiny comes from two rather different sources, which in turn have a bearing on the ways that the politics of gender in the British Army are understood in civil society.

One type of scrutiny is that undertaken by public organisations with a statutory (or government-initiated) responsibility for the oversight of military issues. In the UK, one source is the parliamentary system, through parliamentary debates, and through the parliamentary committee system, where the activities of the Ministry of Defence (MoD) are examined through the work of the defence committees of the Houses of Lords and Commons. These all-party committees have the power to initiate inquiries, question witnesses and demand evidence. Indeed, they are valuable sources of information about military matters when examined alongside information emanating from the armed forces and Ministry of Defence. Another source of scrutiny is the National Audit Office, the government's auditor, which regularly examines specific projects and wider patterns of departmental spending in terms of their value for money. Other sources include non-governmental public bodies that have an interest in the operations of the armed forces. The Equal Opportunities Commission and the Commission for Racial Equality are prominent here, but we would also include the scrutiny offered by organisations, which, from time to time, are prompted to examine various aspects of military life; see, for example, the report on training issues published by the Adult Learning Inspectorate (ALI) in 2005 (which we discuss in Chapter 3). Public organisations with a statutory duty or similar are a crucial part of the mechanism through which the armed forces in the US become publicly accountable. Similar systems of public scrutiny for the sake of accountability operate in other advanced democracies.

Another source of scrutiny is that provided by the media. This is a vitally important source of information and commentary on the armed forces, although its level of engagement and degree of influence will vary enormously with type of media (whether broadcast, print or electronic, and whether corporate or independent), with the audiences and markets to which a particular outlet is orientated, and with the levels of access to defence information granted to an outlet. Media engagement with military matters is a complex and contested issue. Thussu and Freedman[12] identify three narratives or models of media engagement in communicating conflict: the media as critical observer, the media as publicist, and media as a constituent part of the battle space. We can see these three narratives in media coverage not just of conflict, but also of wider defence issues, including coverage of gender issues and defence issues when gender is implicated as an explanatory variable. Media scrutiny, then, is a complex issue that goes far beyond the role of various forms of media as a source of information for civil society about defence matters. Although that role is significant as the primary mechanism through which most British citizens get to hear about military affairs, we should also emphasise that this type of scrutiny is also constitutive, in that it shapes the terms through which information is made meaningful. We should also recognise the role of new forms of media as a source of scrutiny – online blogs and commentaries, for example – which facilitate the public airing of once-private observations of serving soldiers, and which overlap with more traditional forms of information transmission, such as print media.

Both sources of scrutiny affect civilian understandings of military gender issues. Public scrutiny from statutory and other officially recognised organisations carries with it the weight of informed opinion and authority that stems from that government-sanctioned role. This observation holds whether one concurs or disagrees with that body's observations and conclusions. The key point is that official scrutiny and commentary acts as one of the mechanisms by which military gender issues become civilian issues; the very act of a politician stating, for example, that 'the public wouldn't tolerate it' in debates about women's participation in direct combat throws that issue firmly into the public domain. Similarly, observations, such as those of the ALI, that bullying practices tacitly accepted within the forces would amount to gross misconduct subject to instant dismissal outside the forces, raise the disparity between civilian and military practices and pose questions about that difference.[13] Media scrutiny similarly works to place military matters into the public domain, for consideration by the taxpayer. However, media scrutiny is different in outcome. Media scrutiny is constitutive and representational, in that it is through the reporting on and scrutiny of defence issues that those issues are constructed as matters for public concern and debate. This is significant when it comes to considering gender issues; gender issues become civilian issues through media coverage, but as part of the process those issues are moulded and shaped and given meaning; media commentary is discursive rather than reflective.[14]

The second reason why military gender issues are significant as civilian issues follows from this, and relates to the use of the armed forces as a focus, target or repository for wider concerns and anxieties around social issues within civilian society. It is important to at least speculate about the practices that feed this process. Broadcast, print and news media are crucial in this respect. These media forms are perennially interested in gender issues in the armed forces.[15] We would speculate that this reflects not only the transmission of news (negotiations around gender policies are quite rightly publicised through press releases by the MoD), but also the construction of news. Gender stories in the military become news not just because things happen within the armed forces on a day-to-day basis, which duly get reported, but also because gender stories are inherently attractive as news stories. They are attractive because they can readily be retold as human interest stories, an increasingly important mode of news reporting in the contemporary British media, based on the principle that audience or reader identification promotes audience or reader interest and thus circulation and viewing figures. Military gender stories can so easily become people stories, whether they involve sexual transgressors, victims of gendered abuse or heroic examples of military man- and womanhood. Military stories around defence budgets or regimental reorganisation do not have the same allure, even if they are ultimately of far wider structural or operational significance to the armed forces. Military stories can be retold as gender stories for other purposes (and we discuss this in Chapter 4).[16] For example, the personal narrative of US Army prisoner-of-war Melissa Rathbun-Nealy held much less news value within the US print media than speculative narratives about her potential for sexual violation.[17]

Whether the armed forces enjoy or encourage this practice or not, civilian anxieties about changing gender roles, gender relations and gender identities are frequently projected on to the armed forces. It is not difficult to understand why this happens; as an institution identified in the national cultural imagination as embodying a specific form of gender relations revolving around the prioritisation of the masculine and the celebration of particular (and hegemonic) attributes of masculinity, the armed forces become an obvious focus when civilian interest is sparked by wider social shifts in gender relations and gender identities. Furthermore, given the significance of the armed forces in the construction of ideas around national identity, this process of projection around gender is reinforced when combined with concerns about nationhood and national identity. Wider civilian anxieties are mapped on to debates about the armed forces, because the armed forces are so important as part of the nation's cultural imaginary. Social unease about difficult gender questions can be made sense of with reference to the armed forces; they are positioned as a medium through which gender politics are worked out and function as a signifying system for social relations around gender. Military gender issues become civilian issues in this way.

We can illustrate this with reference to examples where this projection process can be seen in operation. A prime example is public anxieties about working mothers – more correctly, mothers who work outside the home in paid employment. In advanced capitalist economies, public debates around the rise in the second half of the twentieth century in the proportion of women with dependent children working outside the home have been structured around concerns for the physical welfare and emotional well-being of the children of these mothers. These debates have been mapped directly on to discussions about the deployment of military personnel. US media interest in the deployment of women soldiers during the 1991 Gulf War and the 2003 (and ongoing) Iraq invasion focused in particular on the position of these women as mothers, raising questions about the care of dependents left behind, particularly for mothers who were sole parent. Needless to say, this was not an issue that male soldiers who were fathers were over-burdened with, despite being a higher proportion of the sole parents in the US military.[18] Women soldiers, their specificity already marked out by their sex, became the repository for much wider public anxieties about working mothers; in many ways, these women were the ultimate working mother, the worker who quite legitimately during the course of doing her job might not come home at the end of her shift.[19]

Another civilian cultural concern similar to this revolves around the feminisation of social, political and economic life – the idea that, with the growth in female economic and political power in advanced capitalist democracies, male privilege has consequently come under challenge. A source of anxiety has been the supposed dissipation of male power as a direct consequence of female empowerment. Again, we can observe how arguments about the feminisation of the social have been mapped on to armed forces through arguments about the feminisation of the military. The feminisation of the military thesis asserts that the increased proportion of women in the military has brought with it a number of problems, which, in combination, undermine military operational capability. Operational capability is reduced because military forces are distracted from their central task (the delivery of lethal force) by what are presented as a range of new obligations that women (it is argued) bring with them.[20] This 'feminisation of the military' argument is interesting, not because of any validity in what its proponents argue – as far as we can see, there is scant evidence that the support and services required specifically for women personnel are of such expense and complexity that they undermine the ability of forces to do their job. Military forces have usually been fairly good at providing the support their personnel require, although there is often public and military concern about the extent to which governments support them in doing so. What is interesting about the 'feminisation of the military' argument is the way in which wider social anxieties about female power and autonomy, including a political agenda that verges on the anti-feminist, are projected onto armed forces, which, as male-dominated institutions adapting to female participation, provide an easy location for arguments that are critical of female advancement.

Gender issues in the military, then, are not just issues for armed forces themselves, but issues of legitimate concern for wider civil society. Civilian understanding is necessary, for reasons of both public accountability and cultural comprehension. We should add that, in our view, writing as civilian academics, engagement with military issues (whether around gender or anything else) is an act of citizenship. Whether or not we endorse the operations that our armed forces are called upon by government to perform, they are our armed forces. Given that the operations they perform in our name may entail danger and the risk of injury or death, there is, in our view, a moral imperative on all of us as civilians to engage with military institutions, to understand what they do and why they do it, and for that engagement to be informed by as full an understanding as we can reach (as civilians) of the reasons why our armed forces are what they are and do what they do.

Conceptualising the politics of gender and the contemporary British Army

The study of gender issues in contemporary armed forces is marked above all else by variety, in approach, focus, conceptual motive and political intention. That variety is evident in the fact that the study of gender is not the preserve of any one academic discipline. Across the humanities, social sciences, the arts and medical sciences, men and women's military participation has exerted fascination and promoted academic scrutiny, for one reason or another. A number of different epistemologies have been brought to bear on the issue, from positivist approaches seeking explanation in statistical patterns with reference to an observable reality, through to interpretative approaches orientated towards the investigation of the discourses through which social life and social practices are given their meaning. The political intentionality of analysts varies enormously, from the modelling exercises of a military sociology allied very clearly with the objectives and intentions of armed forces, to the critical inquiry of emancipatory theory.[21] Within theoretical approaches, there is also considerable diversity and difference. For example, although feminist scholarship and politics as a whole has been enormously influential in marking out the question of women's military participation as a legitimate area for inquiry, there is considerable difference of opinion within feminist theory about the political objectives of such inquiry. Indeed, it makes more sense to talk of the plurality of feminist approaches, given the gulf that exists between, for example, liberal feminist approaches seeking equity for female military participants in an otherwise unchallenged male domain, and radical or different feminist approaches offering an analysis of women's subordination under the military system. How gender is conceptualised varies from studies that perceive gender primarily as an issue of female participation to studies that understand gender as equally an issue for men and for women as they construct, perform and contest military gender identities.[22]

The theoretical approach underpinning the analysis presented here is informed by critical and feminist post-structuralist theory. As Sandra Whitworth notes, critical theory 'rejects the positivist claim that research and theory-making are, or should be, value-neutral activities'.[23] She argues:

> Critical theorists also reject the positivist claim that knowledge can be read off a 'world out there' in an unmediated fashion. They reject, in other words, the idea of an objective reality that can be understood through simple observation. The material conditions of people's lives are important and must be documented, but knowledge about the world and all human activity also is produced through the discursive practices associated with particular phenomena, issues and events. This means that ideas matter.[24]

Feminist theory, as she points out, notes how the ideas that constitute institutions (and indeed nations) are gendered:

> Often those ideas are associated with the exclusion of women and the presence of men, but they are associated also with the *particular* ways both men and women are 'present' in nations, institutions, or events, and the particular expectations associated with both women and men, and masculinity and femininity. Those assumptions, feminists argue, affect how we understand different social phenomena and have an impact on the individual lives of men and women.[25]

The analytic approach we use in this book is based around such an understanding of the significance of ideas and the discourses and language through which they are conveyed. A variety of sources have been used. We have drawn extensively on documentary sources from military institutions. For the analysis that focuses specifically on the British Army, this has meant recourse to documentation on organisational frameworks, policy guidelines and training and operational practices set out in published documentation emanating from the MoD, the Army, the Royal Air Force and the Royal Navy. We have drawn on unrestricted/unclassified documentation, which includes both published (and widely available) documentation and unpublished internal documents of unrestricted classification. These sources include policy background briefings, directives and statements. Documentary sources include publications available on the external (public) websites of these military institutions. Statistical data is drawn from the Defence Analytical Services Agency, an MoD agency. Second, we have drawn also on primary research data, by which we mean data and materials collected by ourselves for research purposes. These data come mostly from semi-structured research interviews conducted with military personnel around the theme of gender and policy in the British Army.[26] In addition, we have drawn on observational data from conversations with military personnel during field research. Where used, the provenance of these data is indicated in endnotes. The anonymity of our respondents has been preserved throughout. Third, we use secondary data sources from previously published research. This includes research monographs and academic texts (books and journal articles). We also draw on unpublished secondary data from research theses and dissertations. Although these are not as widely available as published research, we would note that they constitute an invaluable resource because such data derive from primary research. All sources are acknowledged through footnotes. Fourth, print media sources have been used, less as a source of facts and more as a source for the identification of discourses around gender in the public realm. Television drama has also been used as a source, useful because of the significance of this genre as a site within popular culture for the articulation of arguments around militarism and gender. We also draw on the non-fiction narratives of military memoir, a significant popular cultural form for the communication of military experiences by former soldiers.

Drawing on this analytic approach and these sources, the book is structured as follows. Chapter 2 sets the scene and establishes a historical context, and has been written with the information needs of the interested but non-expert reader in mind. We start by looking at patterns of male and female employment in both the British armed forces and the British Army overall, and then compare the British experience with the armed forces of other nation states. One of the most interesting outcomes of any comparative exercise like this is not in establishing whether or not the British Army is like any other, but rather in establishing which factors make direct comparison so problematic. What becomes clear, once comparisons are attempted, is the contingencies that govern the gendering of military participation. This observation reinforces an emerging consensus within sociological studies of the military, which supports the view that although patterns of gender distribution within armed forces may show similarities across both space and time such diversity is most helpfully explained as an outcome of the social construction of both gender and military activities, rather than any innate and essential difference between men and women. We then go on to put the gendered British Army within a historical context. Drawing on contemporary historiography, we argue that women's military participation has always been accommodated and contained according to the needs of military forces for both male and female labour, clearly seen in the changing patterns of gendered participation over the last 100 years. We also argue, following the work of historians working in this area, that patterns of female participation have continually been shaped to maintain the masculine character of those forces and reflect wider social anxieties about masculinity and femininity, an issue to which we return in later chapters. We take the gendered history of the British Army up to the present and then turn to examine in more detail the patterns of gender differentiation that were signalled at the beginning of the chapter. We look at current personnel data in order to explain where it is, within the Army, that women actually serve, and emphasise through this the internal diversity of an organisation often viewed as a monolithic entity in the public imaginary. We conclude the chapter with some observations about current influences, observed and hypothesised, which affect the present and future gender divisions of military labour in the contemporary British Army.

In Chapter 3 we focus in on women and the construction of female difference within the British Army. Through a reading of a selection of policy initiatives that have had an impact on women's military participation in various ways over the past decade – the expansion of posts open to women, changes in selection and training procedures, the introduction of equal opportunities and diversity strategies, and the exclusion of women from direct combat positions – we show how ideas of female difference from male norms are established and negotiated. We pay particular attention in this chapter not just to the mechanisms that policy initiatives have put in place, but also to the discourses identifiable in the language of policy, which indicate how female difference is constructed. We also try in this chapter to draw connections between Army policy and practice on the one hand and conceptual approaches to understanding women's military participation on the other; we show, for example, how liberal feminist agendas around equity and citizenship issues have impacted on Army gender policy, and how essentialist arguments about male and female differences with respect to war and military activities are echoed in policy discourses around combat participation. We conclude the chapter by considering the latest available research on sexual harassment in the armed forces, research that would appear to contradict a decade of Army claims about equity in opportunity for women (and for ethnic and sexual minorities too) and to support a wider public discourse observing rampant sexism and cultural tolerance of this within the forces. What is clear from this research, and from the armed forces' engagement with it, is a growing realisation in policy circles that cultures of military masculinity, rather than female difference *per se*, lie at the root of difficulties of gender integration.

Chapter 4 takes as its core issue these cultures of military masculinity. The chapter takes as its starting point the growing body of work in social and cultural studies on masculinities, work which has emphasised the significance of the military in the construction of hegemonic masculinities. Within this approach, which is informed by post-structuralist feminist and gender studies that emphasise the embodied, performed and contingent nature of gender identities, a number of influential studies have emerged which point to the necessity of understanding the practices through which masculinities are constructed, perpetuated and challenged. This book is very much a contribution to this approach, and we do this by unpacking some of the attributes and practices of contemporary British military masculinities. These include the performance of heterosexuality, the significance of homosociability and male bonding, the uses of humour, and various bodily practices both officially encouraged and unofficially performed through which male military gender identities are articulated and reproduced. We conclude by speculating on the consequences of these performances of military masculinities for women in the Army, and whether we can observe the emergence of female masculinities in military cultures.

Chapter 5 considers the gendered figure of the soldier more widely in civilian culture. It looks beyond the Army itself, taking as its focus the circulation of ideas around gender and the soldier within popular culture. We examine how the figure of the soldier, male and female, has been imagined, and we do this by looking at both print media and popular television drama, two key sites where the figure of the soldier has been constructed and where anxieties about the soldier and gender have been played out. In particular, we highlight the parallels between discourses about female difference articulated in policy debates on women's military participation, and representations of that difference within popular cultural forms.

Chapter 6 concludes with some observations about the analytic approach taken in the book, which emphasises the significance of discursive practices in how we can understand military institutions. We argue that, although the Army has a material reality, it achieves its form, structure and functions through discourses. If we are properly to understand that institution, we have to understand how it is imagined, brought into being, by discursive practice. We emphasise in particular the practices around the construction of meaning that contain women's military participation and naturalise male masculine practices and performances as part of the construction of gendered military identities. We raise as an issue the consequences of these ideas about the gendered soldier for contemporary social debates around the legitimation of violence.

2 Patterns and histories of gender in the British Army

The British Army is mostly male in its composition, and is widely accepted to be masculine in character. Of its trained personnel, 92 per cent are male. Men and women have always provided the Army with personnel, support and services. That contribution has always been gendered – the division of labour between men and women has never been quantitatively or qualitatively equal. Narratives about gender set out in contemporary military policy discourse, of steadily increasing numbers of women personnel and the expanding opportunities available to them, belie a more complex gendered present and past. The masculine character of the Army is and has always been maintained by a constant process of imagination of the institution as male, and supported consistently by practices, formal and informal, material and cultural, which have contained women's participation and have worked to keep the institution male.

In subsequent chapters, we explore how the masculine character of the Army is maintained through the construction of ideas about female difference in employment policies, through the development of cultures of masculinity that prioritise specific figures and modes of masculinity, and through the circulation of ideas about gender and the military within popular cultural forms that work to reinforce the masculinism of the Army in civilian discourse and culture. The purpose of this chapter is to provide a historical and contemporary context for these explorations of gender. We look at the current gender composition of the British Army and armed forces and discuss this relative to comparator military institutions. Having established a picture of the contemporary gender division of labour, we go on to explore how this has come into being by presenting a gender history of the Army. Our aim is not to provide a comprehensive history of the development of the British Army; there is a rich literature readily available on this giving a level of detail greater than we are able to provide here.[1] Rather, we focus on key points and developments in the Army's past where the politics around sex difference and negotiations over gender relations and identity have most visibly influenced this institution. In the final section, we examine current patterns of sex distribution of Army personnel across the different functional branches of this institution.

Patterns of male and female employment

The British armed forces

In 2006 there were 195,870 trained individuals serving in the British Armed Forces (Army, naval service and Royal Air Force).[2] Of these, 178,000 were men and 17,870 were women. Women constitute a relatively small proportion of the armed forces; about 1 in 10 military personnel are women. A Ministry of Defence (MoD) factsheet posted on its website gives a figure for the proportion of women in the British Armed Forces of 9.1 per cent. The factsheet is celebratory about this proportion, and about its gradual year-on-year increases: 'Today, the contribution of Servicewomen to the combat effectiveness of the Armed Forces is essential. More women are serving in a greater variety of posts than ever before, many of them front line.'[3]

This book is about the Army, being at 107,730 trained strength the biggest of the three armed forces. The same MoD factsheet states that women made up 8.2 per cent of the trained strength of the Army in 2006, although calculations from Defence Analytical Services Agency (DASA) data produce a slightly lower proportion.[4] The latter gives a figure for the Army of 92.40 per cent male (99,550 men) and 7.59 per cent female (8,180 women). In the naval service, out of 39,390 naval personnel, 35,720 are men (90.68 per cent) and 3,680 are women (9.34 per cent). In the Royal Air Force (RAF), out of 48,740 air force personnel, 42,730 are men (87.66 per cent) and 6,010 are women (12.33 per cent). So although across the British Armed Forces women constitute 9.1 per cent trained strength, in the Army they constitute 7.95 per cent. Relative to the other services, they constitute the lowest proportion of personnel, but are present in greater numbers.

There are clear differences between the three armed forces in terms of their gender profiles on the basis of rank.[5] In the Army, 10.8 per cent of officers are women, as are 7.1 per cent of 'other ranks'. In the Navy, 8.7 per cent of officers are women as are 9.4 per cent of other ranks. In the RAF, 13.6 per cent of officers are women as are 11.9 per cent other ranks. Women constitute a higher proportion of officers in the RAF than in the Army, and the lowest proportion of other ranks in the Army compared with the other armed forces.

International comparisons

Comparisons between the British armed forces and those of other nation states are useful, for two reasons. First, given the increasing use of multinational forces for military and constabulary (peace-keeping) operations and, given the recognition of the future significance of interoperability in current MoD policy and planning, arguably the real utility of comparative gender analysis derives from its relevance to operational issues. Interoperability rests in part on shared understandings of force organisation and culture, and this includes an understanding of the utility of men and women's military contributions. Second, an exercise in comparison will show fairly readily the factors that come into play in shaping force differences.[6]

An examination of those not only demonstrates their sheer range across cultural, political, social and economic spheres of military life, and the ways in which they have a bearing on sex distributions and the gendering of forces, but also reinforces the significance of national military and civilian cultural understandings of gender in explaining the male dominance in armed forces cross-nationally.

A broad indication of the cross-national variety between armed forces and armies in terms of their deployment of men and men is contained in data collected annually by the North Atlantic Treaty Organisation (NATO) Committee on Women in the NATO forces. These data, showing the proportions of military forces that are female in NATO members, are given in Table 2.1. This shows the huge disparity between, for example, the Latvian and Hungarian armed forces, in which respectively 18.2 per cent and 17.5 per cent of personnel are women, and the Italian and Polish forces, respectively at 1.6 per cent and 0.5 per cent. The armed forces of the UK, USA, Canada and the Netherlands stand between these two extremes at 9.1 per cent, 10.4 per cent 12.8 per cent and 9 per cent respectively.[7] Looking beyond NATO, the Royal New Zealand Defence Force in

Table 2.1 Women as a percentage of the armed forces of NATO member states

Belgium	8.3
Bulgaria	6
Canada	12.8
Czech Republic	12.2
Denmark	5.3
France	13.28
Germany	6
Greece	5.4
Hungary	15.56
Italy	1.6
Latvia	18.2
Lithuania	12.5
Luxembourg	5.71
Netherlands	9
Norway	7
Poland	0.52
Portugal	12.00
Romania	5
Slovakia	7.7
Spain	13.47
Turkey	3.1
United Kingdom	9.1
United States	10.49

Source: Committee on Women in the NATO forces (2006) *Annual Country Reports*, available at: http://www.nato.int/issues/women_nato/index.html, accessed 30 October 2006.

(The data for Slovenia are absent from the original table. Iceland does not have its own Army, although it contributes assistance to humanitarian missions.)

2000 was about 14.5 per cent female and 13.3 per cent of the Australian Defence Force in 2004 were women.[8] In the South African National Defence Force in 2002, women constituted 20 per cent of the overall force.[9] Less than 1 per cent of the Zimbabwean Defence Force were female.[10] About 4 per cent of the Mexican armed forces were female at the beginning of the twenty-first century.[11] In 2001, women constituted 1.6 per cent of the South Korean armed forces, 4.2 per cent of the armed forces of Japan, 4.5 per cent of the armed forces of China and 2.1 per cent of the armed forces of Taiwan.[12]

However, comparisons between the British armed forces and other militaries are tricky, because the methods for counting and organising national armed forces vary so greatly, as do their fundamental purposes in relation to national defence and international operations. In terms of data collection, different national forces use different strategies for the enumeration of personnel, including how military personnel are actually defined, whether this includes trained and untrained personnel, whether this includes standing forces or reserves, and whether it distinguishes between volunteers and conscripts. For example, the aggregate figure given in Table 2.1 showing women as 13.28 per cent of the French armed forces includes women employed in the procurement agency and health and oil supply services.[13] The figure for the proportion of women in the French Army is much lower, at 9.98 per cent. Differing methodologies for defining and enumerating personnel mean that we should be cautious in what we infer from seemingly straightforward comparisons of proportion.

The organisation of armed forces is also a factor making straightforward comparisons problematic. There are significant differences between forces manned by conscription and those that are all volunteer. Conscript forces may call up both men and women (as the Israeli Defence Force does[14]) or just young men. As many European armed forces change from conscript to all-volunteer forces (France, Italy and Portugal have done so since the end of the 1990s), so too do the relative proportions of men and women.[15] Furthermore, most armies have recourse to reserve forces, and these will vary with size and role, and with expectations about the gender of reservists; the Swiss Army, for example, has an extremely large male reserve reflecting the incorporation of the citizenry into civil defence functions. Organisationally, there are also differences in gender distributions dictated by the roles that women and men are permitted to perform. Some armies allow both men and women in to join infantry and other units defined around direct combat functions. Amongst NATO members, the Canadian, French, Czech, Belgian, Luxembourg, Danish, Hungarian, Norwegian, Spanish, German, Polish, Italian, Slovenian and Bulgarian armies all permit female entry to combat posts, as do the New Zealand and South African armies. The armies of the UK, Australia, the Netherlands, Portugal, Slovakia, Romania, Latvia, Lithuania and the US do not. Amongst armies that restrict female participation in posts defined as combat positions, there are variations; the US Army excludes women from employment in posts where units below brigade level might engage in direct ground combat, and this includes artillery and combat engineer functions.[16] The British Army excludes women from the infantry and the Royal Armoured Corps (tank regiments), but permits them to hold jobs in the artillery and engineers. The reasons for exclusion differ too; the British exclusion is made on the grounds of unit cohesion, and this exclusion has been upheld through British and European legal judgements. The same European legal framework on employment equity facilitated the opening up of combat positions in the German Bundeswehr.[17] The existence of European legislation on employment equity initiated the inclusion of women in the Austrian armed forces because of Austria's need to comply with European Union (EU) legislation following that state's accession to EU membership in 1995.[18]

The defence and national security objectives of the state will also shape the structure and functions of national armed forces and men and women's roles therein. Does an armed force exist purely for national defence or is it perceived to have an international role? How is that international role conceptualised? The British and US armed forces, for example, are understood as (and therefore structured as) forces capable of offensive actions overseas. Other forces see their international roles in more constabulary terms, as contributors to international peace-keeping, peace support and humanitarian interventions, or as purely defensive forces for national territory. The Dutch armed forces, it has been argued, have assumed a self-image of non-martial or unheroic behaviour, a reflection of the prominence of peace-keeping rather than offensive roles in defining its existence.[19] The Danish government, for example, is (at the time of writing) in the process of adopting United Nations (UN) resolution 1325 on women, peace and security, examining how the Danish armed forces can improve the protection of women where its forces are deployed, and facilitate their involvement in post-conflict resolution and reconstruction. This is indicative of gender mainstreaming at the heart of national debates about defence in Denmark, evident in the emphasis within its NATO briefing on women of peace-keeping and peace support operations. National defence and security objectives – what a state thinks its armed forces are actually for – in turn shapes how a state structures its forces and enables or inhibits participation by its population.

Comparisons between armed forces also have to account for how past national and political military histories have shaped contemporary structures and organisation. For example, the UK, French and German armies have all had very different organisational and deployment histories in the period following the end of the Second World War, whatever the similarities between these forces in terms of their experiences of the First World War and their origins as imperial expeditionary forces in the nineteenth century. From 1945, the US maintained a standing army very much in its wartime format, whereas the French Army was remodelled and the German Army completely disbanded following defeat and partition of the German state, to be reinstituted a decade later.[20] The national imaginary underpinning these three armed forces is therefore very different. The South African National Defence Force (SANDF), established in post-apartheid South Africa in 1994, has roots both in the South African Defence Force of the apartheid state and in Umkhonto we Sizwe, the paramilitary wing of the African National Congress (ANC). Many women (predominantly black African women) joined the SANDF with experience of military engagement against the apartheid regime, and brought with them expectations about their ability to be employed in combat posts, reflecting the emancipatory identity politics of the ANC. This explains why the SANDF allows the participation of women in combat positions.[21] National cultural traditions and conventions that draw tight distinctions between male and female social roles will be reflected in expectations about what is appropriate or otherwise for men and women in military roles; see, for example, a study of cultures of gender in Zimbabwe and Mexico, where divisions of male and female labour that equate men with public roles and women with the domestic can be seen to shape the participation of women in the contemporary forces of these two nation states, despite histories in both countries of revolutionary struggle based on emancipatory politics.[22] Social conventions and national imaginations around the existence of the nation state intertwine with military and political histories to shape participation in ways that will differ in degree and outcome between different national armies. Commentators on the gender divisions of labour within the Israeli army and defence forces, for example, emphasise the significance of the military in shaping national identity, particularly the notion of Israel as a 'nation-in-arms', the gendering of this discourse around the idea of the male Jewish Israeli defender, the elision of the warrior ideal with particular ideas about military masculinity, and the consequences of this discourse for the ways in which Israeli women are deployed within the Army both as conscripts and as full-time members.[23]

But, despite this variation in the participation rates of men and women in different national forces around the world, the point remains that armed forces remain male dominated and masculine. What are we to make of this? One line of argument explains the persistence of this gender order as a reflection of innate differences between men and women.[24] There is certainly a degree to which the physical differences between men and women filter through to the military gender division of labour. These physical differences between men and women are often but not exclusively incorporated within wider arguments, which see men and women as essentially different in their attitudes towards armed conflict, a factor which for some lies at the root of the military gender division of labour. There is a broad literature here across a continuum from extremes of anti-feminist polemic to radical or difference feminist thought.[25] These arguments have a tendency to construct women as naturally more peace loving, or influenced by maternalist thinking that makes them less readily able to take life, or look at women's actions in terms of their (unwitting and uninitiated) support for militarism.[26] Men, in contrast, are portrayed as innately more aggressive.

Although we are not dismissing these arguments out of hand – they need to be seen as contributions to ongoing debates rather than final adjudications that are 'right' or 'wrong' – we would argue that current debates on women's military participation and the gendering of the military should be moved on, for three reasons. First, such arguments have little to say about women who choose of their own free will to participate in the military. As Katerina Agostino notes, 'to assert that all women, in the Services or otherwise, need to take back their support of the military is to ignore the economic and emotional ties of many women.'[27] Many women enjoy personally fulfilling and financially rewarding military careers: '[a]re these women to feel morally obliged to leave because ideologically they are supporting an oppressive patriarchal structure?'[28] Ironically, given the influence of liberal feminist discourse and politics in pushing equity agendas in the armed forces, some military women have a stated ambivalence towards feminist politics when the latter becomes equated with radical feminist agendas.[29] Second, as Titunik and others have observed, particularly in the case of the US military, participation in armed forces gives many women opportunities for greater economic stability and social status than they would otherwise have in civilian life; this is particularly the case for women of colour, who constitute around one-half of all enlisted female personnel in the US Army.[30] Third, essentialist arguments, whether proposed by anti-feminist traditionalists or difference feminists, assume a necessary link between gender and military participation. Bob Connell, one of Anglophone sociology's most prolific and incisive theorists of masculinities, has been critical of feminist writings predicated on assumptions about the inherent predatory nature of men and their innate predisposition towards violence.[31] If this is the case, he argues, patriarchy comes to be conceptualised as a set of power relations flowing from men's inner nature, and patriarchy's status as a social and historical construct becomes obscured. Furthermore, essentialist arguments about men and women's inherent natures imply that men can be excused from their actions because their innate masculinity absolves them from personal responsibility.

The connections between gender and military participation, for these reasons, have to be seen as contingent and social in nature, rather than innate, natural, or biological. Joshua Goldstein phrases this best when he argues that the stability and persistence of the gendered military division of labour, attributable to the cultural reproduction of gender roles, produces and reinforces a gender division of labour which, because of the omnipresence of armed conflict across human history in time and space, has become self-perpetuating:

> killing in war does not come naturally for either gender, yet the potential for war has been universal in human societies. To help overcome soldiers' reluctance to fight, cultures develop gender roles that equate 'manhood' with toughness under fire. Across cultures and through time, the selection of men as potential combatants (and of women for feminine war support roles) has helped shape the war system. In turn, the pervasiveness of war in history has influenced gender profoundly – especially gender norms in child-rearing.[32]

He is clear, then, that the military division of labour is social in origin, and that it is shaped not only by military demands, but also by the effects and demands of armed conflict on the wider structure and dynamics of the civilian host population. This is an argument with which we concur.

A gender history of the British Army

Male domination, then, is a feature of most national armed forces. In this section, we look at how this gender division of labour has evolved over time. Our core argument here is that, although the British Army has always been male dominated, that dominance has never been absolute. As Lucy Noakes has argued, the British Army has incorporated female labour when it has needed it, but has contained female participation because of cultural pressures within the Army to maintain the masculine character of that force, and because of wider social pressures on the Army for the maintenance of social conventions about men and women's social roles.[33]

Regular armed forces, in a form that we would recognise now, emerge in tandem with the establishment of the modern nation state, one feature of which is the monopoly over the deployment of lethal force. Modern nation states are usually recognised as emerging during the mid-seventeenth century.[34] Although the capacity to raise troops and wage war had always been available to the political elites in pre-modern Europe, such forces were irregular, locally raised militias or mercenary armies. It is with the establishment of the New Model Army of the parliamentary period and the consolidation of irregular forces in order to fight the Dutch under the restored Stuart monarchy that we see the roots of the modern Army. Indeed, some British regiments tell a history that dates back to this time, but none goes earlier.[35] Organised armed forces are a feature of modernity; with the advent of an industrialised manufacturing capability, and a state ambition to develop and secure markets overseas, a regular armed force was required during the eighteenth century to serve these ends, on land and at sea. The British Army was established as an instrument of state ambitions that were global in reach.

We know little about these early English and later British armies in terms of their gender dynamics.[36] We know that they drew on both men and women, but in the absence of documentary evidence we should be cautious about sweeping statements judging these either as all-male or as gender-integrated forces. The evidence that we have suggests that female military participation was structured according to the gender roles and conventions dominant at the time, with women providing catering, laundry welfare and nursing services to their men folk (although male camp followers provided these services too).[37] The derogatory term 'camp follower' used in the English language today reflects ambivalence about the roles performed by this parallel army, roles that included sexual services. Much of what we know about women in the armies of the eighteenth century comes from the stories of specific women whose histories by virtue of their exceptionalism have been transmitted to the present.[38]

The British Army in the nineteenth century

The British Army of the nineteenth century was essentially structured around the British state's colonial and imperial project, the physical expression of the state's strategic attempts to dominate markets and resource-rich territories beyond the island of Britain. The colonial and imperial ambitions of the state required an expeditionary army able to travel, fight and garrison in British colonies around the world, the campaigns of which were targeted at the containment of competitor nation states whose own objectives were interpreted as inimical to British strategic interests. Many of these engagements were obscure at the time and forgotten now, but others live on in popular consciousness because of the wider social impacts they precipitated, or because their memory is preserved in forms that speak to us still today. The defeat of French forces under Napoleon at Waterloo in 1815 by an alliance of Prussian and British forces, for example, facilitated British territorial expansion in the early nineteenth century unchecked by French competition, and has also become a synonym in the English language for a decisive defeat. The engagement of British troops in the Crimea (1854–6) in alliance with French troops against Russian expansion into Turkey is notable today less for any enduring gains brought by that engagement and more for the military reforms that the Crimean debacle precipitated. The Indian Mutiny (1857–8), a rebellion against British colonial mercantile power, brought in the wake of military repression the formal militarised state control of Indian territory and the establishment of the British Raj.

The enlisted Victorian army of early and mid-nineteenth century Britain was largely an unpopular institution, a body of poorly paid men who enlisted for life, often against their will or better judgement, in the absence of any other alternatives. Female participation in this expeditionary force was extremely limited. Political distrust of a standing army run by professional soldiers was such that commissions were granted only to those who could purchase them, which opened up the Army as a career for gentlemen of independent means but little ability for anything else. Poorly organised, overstretched and (with notable exceptions) inadequately led, the campaigns such as those in the Crimea and India were notable for the high loss of life from disease and malnutrition as much as from injuries and fatalities of the battle field. In turn this prompted major reforms of the British Army under the Cardwell reforms of the 1870s and the Childers reforms of the 1880s, which, combined, are credited with establishing the foundations for the army that served the British state in two world wars. For example, under the Cardwell reforms, the Department of War was reorganised and we see here the emergence of an efficient civil service providing organisational support and established mechanisms for communication between government and the military. The Army Enlistment Act of 1870 cut soldiers' basic term of service to 12 years. Pay and conditions were improved and the flogging of offending soldiers in peacetime was abolished. Potential officers were no longer reliant on the purchase of commissions, and this period of reorganisation marks the start of a process of professionalisation in the officer corps. Regiments were given formal links with shire counties and localities across Britain, consolidating geography of regimental association with place that still continues, albeit in different forms. Uniform changes, initiated in India in the 1880s with the replacement of red coats with khaki ones, continued through to the end of the century; khaki (a Hindi word of Sanskrit origin, meaning dust coloured) is now synonymous with the British Army. Although organisationally reformed, the socially ambivalent position of the common soldier remained, expressed for example in Rudyard Kipling's poem *Tommy*, published in 1892: 'Yes makin' mock o' uniforms that guard you while you sleep / Is cheaper than them uniforms and they're starvation cheap.'[39] The expeditionary force sent to South Africa to secure British control over territory and resources (the Boer War, 1899–1902) drew soldiers from across the Empire to shore up a British volunteer Army that eventually numbered a quarter of a million men and a considerable number of women as nurses.[40] The weapons and tactics of fighters for the Boer republics inflicted heavy losses on this large force, bringing many British families into contact with distant war through the losses the fighting inflicted. The Boer War is also significant in British social history because the call-up of men of fighting age revealed quite explicitly the poor state of physical health of this volunteer body of men, a consequence of lives of hard and poorly rewarded labour, malnutrition and ill health caused by poverty, inadequate housing and public health services, and low levels of basic education. Reforms that followed in the early twentieth century centred around the establishment of a small but relatively well-equipped British Expeditionary Force, supported by a new territorial army or special reserve replacing older volunteer and yeomanry forces. Recruitment rates were low, but the mass conscription of adult men was resisted politically. The Haldane reforms of 1907 also brought into being organisations which formalised women's military participation in nursing and auxiliary roles, with the establishment of the First Aid Nursing Yeomanry (FANY) and of the Voluntary Aid Detachment (VAD) in 1908.[41]

Our contemporary knowledge of female military participation across this period is shaped by two distinct approaches to gender in military history. One approach emphasises that this is a period in which exceptional women stand out on the basis of their individual contributions to a wider war effort that is largely male. Florence Nightingale, an upper class Englishwoman of independent means, continues to be celebrated as she was during her lifetime for her efforts to improve standards of hygiene and health amongst the diseased soldier–victims of the Crimean campaign. Mary Seacole, her contemporary, has been reclaimed in the late twentieth century not only as a campaigner of equivalent significance for her work improving the health and welfare of soldiers serving in the Crimea, but also as a significant reminder of the often forgotten role played by the wider Empire's subjects in contributing to the British state's military efforts.[42] Furthermore, our contemporary fascination with the transgression of gender roles is evident in the celebration of remarkable women who, through recourse to disguise and subterfuge, served alongside their male compatriots in military roles. The celebration of exceptional women, identifiable in small numbers and made visible through the atypicality of their achievements, dominates narratives of gender and military participation in the eighteenth and nineteenth centuries.[43] These histories are illuminating about the gendered roles demanded of military service and domestic relations in the colonial armies of the nineteenth century with their periods of foreign service and family separation.[44]

Another approach has been to understand men and women's military participation in the context of the production and reproduction of dominant ideas of masculinity and femininity, and the ideas or imagination of Britain and Empire articulated through gender. Lucy Noakes, for example, drawing on the work of Graham Dawson and Michael Paris, contextualises her history of the early formalised contribution of women to the British Army within a later nineteenth-century cultural celebration of war expressed through a popular militarism and 'pleasure culture' in war.[45] She argues that popular culture at the time worked to glamorise and romanticise war through representations of war as chivalric and heroic, in comparison with the mundane pleasures and privations of daily life. This romanticised image of war, consolidated for example through literature, through popular print media aimed increasingly at young people, and through a culture of muscular Christianity celebrated in elite education, encouraged a popular militarism, which, in turn, countered more subversive or radical views of the army as an agent of social control.

The First World War, 1914–18

The British Expeditionary Force dispatched to Belgium and northern France in the late summer of 1914 was supposed to be one of the best that left the shores, and the anticipated short skirmish was expected to be over by that Christmas. The force that set sail comprised six infantry divisions and one cavalry division, numbering about 247,400 personnel. It suffered severe losses during the first months of war, as did its French and Russian allies and the opposing German forces, but maintained a territorial hold in northern Europe facing the opposing German forces along a line, the Western Front, that famously stretched south from the French and Belgian coasts to the Swiss border. The fighting of the First World War was characterised by mass carnage on both sides along this basically static line, marked by complex systems of trenches occupied by forward forces on both sides and separated by no-man's-land in between. The First World War is the first modern industrial war, a total war in which systems of national mobilisation focused a nation's efforts on the mobilisation and supply of men and matériel to feed the efforts of troops on the front line. The call for volunteers started with the declaration of war, with Field Marshall Kitchener (famously depicted on a recruitment poster pointing to the reader and proclaiming that 'Your country needs you!') rebuilding the Army to the extent that 1,186,000 men of fighting age and ability had enlisted by the end of 1914 and 2.5 million by the end of 1915. In our contemporary histories of that early period of the First World War, mass male voluntary enlistment is ascribed to the popular purchase of both patriotic ideals of military service for the nation and the wider British Empire, and of ideals of masculinity as naturally martial in origin. The forces under British command entrenched along the Western Front were truly international, reflecting the reach of Empire and the consequent ability of the British state to enlist in its Army's ranks soldiers from its overseas dominions – India, Australia, New Zealand, Canada, Africa and the Caribbean. High rates of fatalities and casualties, however, made conscription necessary to ensure a continued supply of fit fighting bodies, and this was introduced in January 1916 through the Military Service Act, which applied to single men aged 18–41 years. In May 1916, conscription was extended to married men, and in April 1918 conscription was further extended to men up to the age of 50. In total, about 5 million men served in the British Armed Forces during this Great War.

Women were participants too, working primarily in service support roles in a range of organisations, which vary in our contemporary public memories from the famous to the obscure.[46] The principal organisations deploying female labour were the First Aid Nursing Yeomanry (FANY) and the Voluntary Aid Detachment (VAD), similar in their provision of primarily nursing care and medical assistance to the military wounded, but distinct in their respective organisational position, ethos and the class composition of their members. The VAD also provided other service support such as catering assistance. In the summer of 1914 over 47,000 women worked within the VAD in Britain, rising to 82,000 by 1920, and women members were posted across the theatres of combat including the Western Front, Gallipoli (in what is now modern Turkey) and Mesopotamia (in what is now modern Iraq). In early 1917, the Women's Auxiliary Army Corps (WAAC) was established, a mechanism for deploying female labour in selected areas (cookery, mechanics, clerical and medical roles), thus freeing male labour for military service elsewhere – usually the front line of battle. The establishment of the WAAC was contested at the time, despite the value of this added, organised body of workers to the war effort; the Chief Controller Helen Gwynne-Vaughan is quoted as remarking 'I discovered that the objection to the employment of women was almost universal.'[47] The WAAC was renamed the Queen Mary's Army Auxiliary Corps in April 1918. Around 57,000 women volunteered their services through this Corps, of whom about 6,000 were based in France. Although the nursing and ambulance-driving women of the First World War figure in popular histories of this conflict, other smaller outfits do not. Commenting on preparations for its major 2003–4 exhibition on women and war, a representative of the Imperial War Museum emphasised to us the efforts to which the curators had gone to secure at least a mention of the many small organisations that had drawn on female labour during the First World War. Such organisations included the 2,000-strong Almeric Paget Military Massage Corps, whose staff provided therapeutic massage to the wounded in France towards the end of the war, the Women's Forage Corps, which maintained the supply of horse fodder for an Army reliant on horsepower, and the Women's Forestry Corps, which helped produce wood for paper and timber production.

There is any number of possible observations about the consequences for gender relations and gender identities of the First World War; we limit ourselves to three. First, there has been considerable debate amongst historians about the emancipatory potential of that war for British women.[48] The participation of women in the waged labour market in both traditional (service and support) and less traditional (industrial) occupations has been interpreted as offering a range of new opportunities to women hitherto limited by the gender segmentation of the labour market and by social conventions around gender roles. War, for many, was an emancipatory experience. This broad observation, however, conceals great disparities of experience amongst British working women at the time, marked along lines of class. Although for some women entry into the waged labour market was a novel experience, for those recruited into manual industrial and agricultural sectors the experience of war work was less of a profound change in personal circumstances and experiences and more an exchange of one type of waged labour (such as domestic service) for another. Noakes argues persuasively that to understand the Great War's impact on gender relations and gender identities we have to frame our understanding around the idea that the British Army accommodated women in order to draw on their labour, while simultaneously maintaining a forces identity as masculine; women's labour and contribution was therefore tightly controlled and highly contained around specified military service and support functions. When the requirement for labour diminished following the Armistice, and demobilisation proceeded in the immediate aftermath, women's labour was no longer required, and for many women opportunities in the waged labour market were abruptly curtailed. In addition, the containment of women's participation also worked to support politically dominant civilian discourses around masculinity, femininity and the appropriate gender roles expected of men and women.[49] The debates over uniform for women in services attached to the armed forces is an example here, with concerns about the colour and cut of women's uniforms reflecting dominant social ideas about the need to maintain the femininity of women serving alongside the armed forces.

Second, this period is immensely significant in the evolution of feminist politics and feminist thought. The movement for women's suffrage, suspended for the duration of the war, was re-energised after the war with the development of wider arguments about the citizenship rights earned by both men and women through sacrifices made during the war.[50] The roots of contemporary liberal feminism are identifiable here.[51] In addition, in the post-war period, and as a direct consequence of experiences of loss and observations of mass suffering that the war brought about, a feminist pacifism emerged in France, Britain, Germany and the US. Maternalist in much of its rhetoric, this post-war feminism was significant both in drawing connections between militarism and war (a correlation that continues to inspire feminist activism, particularly more radical feminisms) and in providing a foundation for women's wider civic political activism.[52]

Third, this period is also significant for the rupture (or otherwise) brought by this conflict to dominant social understandings in Britain about the male body. The impact of this war on the male body was profound, and has been traced by Joanne Bourke in the discourses surrounding male physical engagement in fighting, and the effects of mutilation and death on contemporary and post-war conceptions of masculinity and its corporeality.[53] Social constructions of masculinity, varying by class as well as with the nature of bodily impact, were remoulded through the experiences of warfare on male flesh. Bourke is particularly interested in the continuities and disruptions to the impact of war had on prevailing ideas about masculinity both during and after the conflict.

The Second World War, 1939–45

In the Second World War, in which the UK engaged with French and American allies in the defeat of German and Italian military power and territorial ambition in both Europe and Africa, and with allies against Imperial Japan in the Far East, the British Army once again expanded. This second twentieth century experience of mass warfare relied on the incorporation of men of fighting age and ability through mass conscription, and drew also on female labour in military and non-military support roles. Although there are parallels between the First and Second World Wars in terms of the incorporation of female labour and the consequences of this for individuals' experiences of war, the Second World War is distinct in two particular ways. First, the military roles and functions required of both men and women reflected new forms of warfare. The use of mobile armoured formations (tanks) and developments in the mobility of artillery and troops facilitated human movement across territory in ways that shifted the spatialities of warfare. The development of technologically sophisticated weaponry heralded the start of a process by which the fighter – as operator of equipment – could operate at a distance from the victim of this equipment's effects. Second, the new ways of waging war, seen in the Second World War in the use of air power and aerial bombardment, blurred distinctions between battlefront and home front in unprecedented ways. Aerial bombardment could be used to destroy opposing armies and the systems of production that supplied these armies, but it could also be used to target civilians through the blanket bombing of urban centres.[54] Non-combatant men and women became participants in war as victims, in ways that continue to the present.

The Second World War was a war of mass participation. Narratives about the war, which emerged during the period of conflict and were sustained in its aftermath, frame the conflict as a 'people's war', in which warfare impacted on civilian life in ways that previous European conflicts had not. People's war it may have been, but those people's roles were still deeply divided along gender lines.[55] Men of fighting age and ability were conscripted, and the Army grew from a body of 1,128,000 and a total for the armed forces of 1,557,000 in December 1939 to an Army of 3,007,300 and armed forces totalling 4,984,300 by April 1945.

In September 1938, prior to the declaration of war, the Auxiliary Territorial Services (ATS), incorporating the FANY, was established. (In 1938 processes enabling male conscription were also put in place.) Eventually enlisting over 200,000 women, the ATS provided the armed forces (still resolutely all male) with service support over a range of functions including orderlies for office work, drivers, postal workers, cooks, police, gun crews and staff for general operational support tasks. As Lucy Noakes documents, the ATS was not initially a popular institution for women available for war work. The ATS was incorporated into the armed forces at the end of 1941, with the result that women were available (if they were willing) for engagement in operational areas. However, women's military participation was not given equal recognition to that of men. Women served, for example, in anti-aircraft batteries, but they received lower rates of pay and remained members of a separate organisation that itself was viewed as lower status.[56]

With legislative changes in 1941, initiated because of labour shortages, women were increasingly directed into employment in industrial and manufacturing sectors. In total, 16.5 million men and women registered for non-military national service during the Second World War. In December 1941, the National Service Act (No. 2) enabled the conscription of both women and men, with single women aged between 19 and 30, and without children, conscripted for war work attached to the armed forces, the Land Army (providing agricultural labour) and industry, including heavy industry and the manufacture of armaments.

We confine ourselves to two observations, amongst many, regarding the gendered division of labour and the consequences for understandings of men and women's participation during the Second World War.[57] The first, as Penny Summerfield and Corinna Peniston-Bird argue, is that the Second World War was an extremely contradictory period for the boundary between male and female roles, during which 'new indicators of the limits of masculinity and femininity were generated, old definitions of what it meant to be a man or a woman were at the same time strengthened, weakened and preserved intact'.[58] They examine the efforts that went towards sustaining an idea of the defence of the 'home front' around gender ideologies through the exclusion of women from the Home Guard, despite the blurring of the distinction between male and female, combatant and non-combatant, aggressor and victim, which the threat and practice of aerial bombardment and the imagination of the threat of invasion provoked. As Lucy Noakes argues, discourses supportive of mass male mobilisation drew on ideas equating male participation with combat and the defence of home and the domestic sphere. Women's contribution was represented as being structured around the home and the nurturing and protection of children.[59] Yet the demands for ideologies equating the male with combatant and as protector of the female, necessary to support mass male mobilisation, had to compete with the demands for mass mobilisation of labour for the war effort, and, as with the First World War, women's labour was utilised both in auxiliary military roles and in non-military civilian labour forces, in order to 'free a man for the Front'. Women's military participation in Britain was contained, restricted to service and combat support roles, and, post war, both in military and civilian spheres, women were demobilised quickly. Yet during wartime, population mobilities and changing social mores around personal relationships, provoked by uncertainties and threats of death, worked to open up new spaces for men and women's social and sexual engagement. War, for many young men and women, was an exciting time because of the instabilities in gender roles that the war entailed. The film *Went the Day Well?*, a fantasy (and propaganda) film made in 1941 centring on the repulsion of a German invasion by the inhabitants of a stereotypical rural village, reflects this. The home front is reconfigured as the front line, and in its defence women engage in acts of violent attack and defence against the invaders, transgressing established gender roles for the greater cause of national defence. Stories that emerged in the aftermath of war, about the activities of individual women deployed in occupied Europe through the Special Operations Executive, continue to fascinate, precisely because their stories are so exceptional. Another narrative is quite the opposite, and is one of reclamation of the stories of ordinary women during extraordinary times.[60] A tradition of documenting ordinary people's lives during wartime, initiated through the mass observation projects, continues.

The Cold War

The profound geopolitical shifts brought about by the Second World War shaped the size, organisation and functions of the post-war Army. The term 'Cold War' is used to describe the period from 1945 to 1990 during which the mass armies of the US and NATO allies (including the UK), and of the Soviet Union and her satellite East European states, engaged in a state of perpetual readiness for a European land war (which included the development of nuclear arsenals on both sides), and engaged militarily, directly and through proxy states, in small-scale conflicts around the world. Although framed in state and popular discourse as a time of peace, this period saw continued engagement by British forces across the spectrum of military operations and around the world, in the Far East (Malaya, Korea) and the Middle East (Aden, Suez). This was also a period of disengagement from Empire as the populations of colonised territories asserted independence and self-determination, and these colonial disengagements were militarily supported, whether that disengagement was contested or acquiesced by the British state.

A state of military readiness against the perceived Soviet threat and the deployments around colonial disengagement both required a mass standing army. Reluctance to remain in the armed forces from civilian conscripts who had enlisted during the war and shortfalls in recruitment of volunteers were both factors in the introduction of National Service under the National Service Act of July 1947.[61] In addition, there were political aspirations around National Service; Ernest Bevin had argued for conscription as a means of democratising Britain. The period of National Service, from 1947 to 1963, marks the only time that the British state has ever conscripted forces in peacetime. National Service was universal for all able-bodied men aged 18–26, who were traced through the tax and health systems and called up. Certain categories of men were exempt – British subjects in government posts abroad, people with mental or physical disabilities, clergymen, coalminers, merchant seamen and seagoing fishermen, agricultural workers, police cadets and graduate science teachers. Deferment was offered to apprentices and students. But beyond these exceptions National Service was an otherwise universal experience for young white British men in the late 1940s and 1950s (young men in Northern Ireland were also exempt). National Service came into force in 1949 and conscripts were required to enlist for one year, later for two, followed by five years' attachment to reserve forces. Enlistment requirements were amended in 1948 to 18 months because of the demands of the Malaya campaign. By 1951, national servicemen accounted for half of the British Army's personnel. The defence review of 1957 following the Suez crisis in 1956 argued for better-armed, more rapidly deployable professional armed forces, and the abolition of National Service. The last intake was in 1960, and the last national serviceman was demobilised in May 1963. In total, 1,132,872 men were conscripted into the British Army through National Service, of whom 395 were killed while on active service.

National Service, quite apart from its uniqueness in peacetime conscription in Britain, is notable in gender terms for two reasons. First, it was a universal experience for almost all young men at the time, and was therefore significant in the development and reproduction of post-war masculinities. David Morgan, himself a national serviceman, notes how post-war civilian masculinities had, as a consequence, strong connections with military models of masculinity. Furthermore, the subcultures and countercultures of the later 1950s and 1960s in Britain could be understood as evolving in opposition to the rigours, disciplines and moralities of military life.[62] Second, this was more than young men's experience; it played out through the integration of military life into daily civilian life and civilian culture. This was 'a military and social phenomenon' which 'shaped the way generations thought'.[63] Most people knew someone, whether through kith or kinship networks, who was away doing National Service, with the corresponding familiarity with military life that was shared and far reaching.[64]

Women of the same age were not conscripted into National Service. Women's military participation in the post-Second World War period took place through the Women's Royal Army Corps (WRAC), established in February 1949.[65] Their participation within military life was limited, with the then Secretary of State for War stating that 'women will, of course, be employed only on work for which they have a special aptitude'.[66] Members of the WRAC were trained for and assigned to operational support tasks, primarily in transport, communications and administration, with 35 different jobs open to them. They were trained and armed but only for self-defence. Female military participation throughout the Cold War period was channelled solely through the WRAC. By the late 1970s, the WRAC numbered around 4,500 regulars and just over 2,000 territorials, and until 1979 constituted 2.5 per cent of the regular Army. From 1982 small arms training was given, and from 1984 some training was integrated. In 1989, women constituted 4.3 per cent of the armed forces. There was, however, an upper quota of 10 per cent on the number of places open to women across the armed forces, although this was removed by European legislation in 1992.[67]

During this time, and unrelated to the superpower stand-off, British troops were deployed in Northern Ireland, initially to assist with the protection of the Catholic population, and subsequently to counter the paramilitary activities of Catholic and Protestant groups. Significantly for both domestic politics and for popular understandings of military roles, British forces engaged with Argentinian forces over the invasion of the Falklands/Malvinas in 1982. The task force that sailed to the South Atlantic was virtually all male, comprising primarily infantry, paratroops and Royal Marines Commandos. Commentaries on the popular cultural construction and representation of this conflict emphasise the distinction between an active male force engaged in armed combat and a passive female population waiting at home for the return of their men folk, and the significance of this conflict in constructions of British national identity in the 1980s.[68]

During this period, although participation within the military labour market was restricted, within wider civilian labour markets women's participation continued to expand, with in an increase in employment rates for women of working age, both part- and full-time. The establishment in Britain of a post-war Welfare State is associated with the expansion of employment opportunities for women in the welfare, health and education sectors. In addition, levels of education for women raised by the accessibility of free universal secondary education to the age of 16 were also significant in expanding the labour market aspirations of certain groups of women. Politically, the 1960s and 1970s were significant for gender relations with the emergence of second-wave feminism as a political force, one eventual outcome of which was the establishment of policies and legislation on equal opportunities for women at work, and equal pay. The 1980s saw the emergence of a female professional elite, with women's rates of participation in professional and managerial roles increasing (albeit within the context of observations about the limits to which they were able to do so). Although the labour market towards the end of the twentieth century in Britain remained structured along lines of ethnicity, gender and class, there is evidence that in terms of gender, in some occupations, women were starting to achieve parity with men to a degree unimaginable 50 years earlier.

The Gulf War, the 1990s and the present

In 1990, Iraq invaded Kuwait. A coalition of forces, led by the US, was deployed to the region and in 1991 a brief land war, preceded by a campaign of air strikes, forced the Iraqi army out of Kuwait and back into Iraq. A British force of 42,000 deployed to the Persian Gulf under Operation Granby; this force included around 1,100 female armed forces personnel, of which the largest proportion was deployed with the Army, where they constituted 2.8 per cent of deployed personnel. At that time, women constituted around 5 per cent of the total trained Army strength. The deployment of women in the 1991 Gulf War was the first deployment of women in armed conflict by British forces since the Second World War, although because of the pattern of female military participation at the time, with participation wholly through the WRAC albeit attached to other arms and corps, the vast majority of these women were stationed in Divisional Rear HQ.[69] Lucy Noakes notes how debates on women's military participation at the time drew on the supposed degradation of women that exposure to the horrors of war was assumed to bring.[70] Public debate on the participation of female US Armed Forces personnel revolved around fears of the violation of the bodies of female prisoners of war, and the violation of the maternal role that the deployment of female parents represented.[71]

The 1991 Gulf War marks the last deployment of the large British Army of the Cold War period. Initiated before this conflict in response to the collapse of the Soviet Union and the dissipation of that threat to mainland Europe, and rolled out following the withdrawal of British troops from the Middle East, the programme of downsizing under *Options for Change* in 1991 reduced the size of the British

Armed Forces by 30 per cent. The WRAC was disbanded, and its personnel incorporated into what became the Adjutant General's Corps, undertaking primarily administrative and personnel functions. Field training was open to women, who were now permitted up to 8 km from the front line, or further forward if role required. A total of 47 per cent of posts in the Army were opened to women, with the exceptions being posts in the infantry, the Royal Armoured Corps (tanks), and engineering and artillery units. In addition, pregnant personnel were now entitled to maternity leave, a marked shift from a policy that allowed pregnant personnel to be sacked; between 1978 and 1990, just under 5,000 women had been dismissed from the armed forces when pregnant. This policy change, instigated under the Treaty of Rome's Equal Treatment Directive, is estimated to have cost the MoD £55 million in payment of compensation claims brought by former personnel.[72]

British armed forces engaged, during the 1990s, in a range of peace support, peace-keeping and humanitarian missions around the world, including Bosnia, Kosovo and Sierra Leone. The restructuring of the armed forces under *Options for Change* and subsequent reviews was based on assumptions that greater flexibility would be required amongst deployed units in terms of the roles they would have to undertake, and that, with an increase in international cooperative missions under the auspices of the UN and NATO, greater interoperability would be required within and between armed forces. Questions about the ability of the armed forces to recruit sufficient numbers from a diminishing pool of potential recruits were addressed through the MARILYN review initiated in 1989 which suggested that recruitment could be encouraged amongst social groups that had hitherto been restricted from or disinclined to participate in the armed forces – groups such as women and members of ethnic minorities.[73] Research conducted at this time also emphasised the difficulties the Army faced in expanding its potential pool of recruits to deal with overstretch; social changes in civilian society and acceptance of differences around gender, sexuality, ethnicity and class needed to be embedded organisationally and addressed culturally within the armed forces, an ongoing issue revolving around the need for military specificity on the one hand and military alignment with civilian society on the other.[74] Later in this period, what Christopher Dandeker terms the 'people dimension' of the UK armed forces becomes much more central in defence planning.[75] We see, for example, the Strategic Defence Review initiative by the incoming Labour Government, published in 1998, establishing an Armed Forces Overarching Personnel Strategy (AFOPS), published in 2000 and providing formal guidance for the development of personnel policies aimed at recruitment and retention of trained personnel across the three armed forces. Significantly in terms of women's participation, in 1998 three arms/corps were opened up to women, raising from 48 per cent to 70 per cent the proportion of posts open to women. Posts in the Royal Artillery (RA), Royal Electrical and Mechanical Engineers (REME) and Royal Engineers (RE) were now open to women soldiers (and we discuss this in more detail in Chapter 3).

There are four significant points about the changes in the British Army initiated from the early 1990s onwards, and which have a bearing on gender relations and the politics of gender within the Army. The first is that there is a significant degree of engagement between the armed forces and external civilian equity agencies over equity and discrimination issues, although the objectives of both parties were different.[76] The Equal Opportunities Commission, for example, through its involvement with individual employment tribunals, brought pressure to bear on the Armed Forces to facilitate institutional changes around the recruitment, selection, training and career management of women personnel (and we cover this in detail in Chapter 3). The second is the explicit recognition in policy that retention issues were also gender issues; AFOPS engaged with family issues as they affected service personnel, a reflection that the morale of deployed troops rests in part on domestic stability.[77] Third, the 1990s marks a period of downsizing in the total manned strength of the British Army, coupled with the outsourcing of many managerial functions through next steps agencies, public private partnerships and private finance initiatives, and the growth (which continues to the present) of private military companies. There have been no definitive studies on the implications of military outsourcing for the deployment of women personnel or for the gender divisions of labour in the new outsourced functions; we can speculate, however, that because of the continued growth of women in (civilian) service sector and managerial occupations this period sees a change in the relative proportions of men and women deployed in defence-related occupations. Fourth, reflecting both operations at that time and changes in defence thinking, the functions of the Army expanded to include organisation explicitly around peace-keeping and humanitarian missions. The consequences for women's deployment are interesting, with debates at this time emphasising the benefits of women's participation for the Army's ability to undertake these tasks.[78] Television advertisements at this time (which we discuss in Chapter 5) were specific to a moment at which for manning and operational reasons women's participation in the Army was actively encouraged. Furthermore, debates around a so-called 'Revolution in Military Affairs', an idea that contemporary land forces could be smaller, rapidly deployable and technologically enabled, were recognised as having implications for women's further deployment. The logic of this assumes that differences in physical capability between men and women were of decreasing importance because technologically sophisticated, weapons-driven modes of modern warfare relied less on the physical abilities of individual soldiers and more on the ability of soldiers to operate complex equipment. According to this logic, physical strength becomes less important than mental ability. The most significant debate at this time, around gender and military participation, concerned the continued exclusion of women from combat posts. In the UK, this debate was re-ignited in 1998, with the opening up of posts in artillery and engineering regiments to women, but was subject to a long review, eventually published in 2002, which confirmed that women would not be allowed into infantry and armoured regiments; we discuss this in more detail in Chapter 3.

As we write, men and women are engaged in military operations in Iraq and Afghanistan. The military response initiated by the US to the attacks in September 2001 in Washington and New York was supported by the British Armed Forces first through interventions in Afghanistan from October 2001 and extended in

2006, and from 2003 through British participation in the invasion of Iraq and the subsequent attempts to establish a change of regime acceptable to the US and her allies. The focus of British defence policy, post 2001, has emphasised, amongst other things, the changing nature of security and the changing nature of armed response. Talk is of rapid assault capabilities, of network-enabled capability, of technological warfare and asymmetric warfare. Gender issues are still visible in policy, in debates about sexual harassment, about extremes of destructive behaviour incompatible with military discipline and attributed to uncontrolled male aggression, and in debates about the relationships between the retention of both male and female personnel and family policies. Worth emphasising too, is the simple observation that, although women are now fully integrated within the British Army, this integration is uneven. We turn now to describe this in greater detail.

Current patterns of sex distribution

The British Army, like any armed force, exists in order to exercise potentially lethal force in support of the political objectives of the British Government. The exercise of force takes many forms and requires the deployment of personnel and weapons in varying configurations and in varying circumstances, whether this is the use of armoured and mechanised infantry to take and control swathes of territory, such as the invasion of southern Iraq by British troops in March and April 2003 or the patrolling presence of British troops in Northern Ireland as a means of controlling insurgent activity, or the deployment of heavy artillery to attack a more distant enemy. The Army uses primarily infantry, tanks and artillery. To do this, communications between units need to be secured. Intelligence is required about opposing forces in order to make rational decisions on the deployment of force. The logistics of supply of soldiers, weapons, ammunition, food and medical resources needs to be worked out. Vehicles require maintenance and repair. The wounded need to be tended. In addition, this organisation of over 100,000 military personnel needs to be administered. In short, this is not a monolithic organisation.

A threefold classification of Army arms and services is helpful in understanding the roles and functions of the various parts of this complex organisation; we can think in terms of combat functions, combat support functions and combat service support functions. Unsurprisingly, there is a gender dimension to this classification. Of the 8,180 women in the British Army, 1 per cent are employed in combat units (all within the Army Air Corps, for which they constitute 4 per cent of the total strength), 21.9 per cent are in combat support units (artillery, engineering, signals, intelligence) and the remaining 77.1 per cent are in combat service support units (policing, logistics, general engineering, personnel, medical and logistics functions).[79] Combat positions are closed to women, are therefore entirely male. As of April 2006, there were 26,290 personnel in the Infantry and 6,030 in the Household Cavalry and Royal Armoured Corps (tanks). Around one-third of the British Army are therefore deployed in posts classified as combat posts.

Combat support and combat service support positions are open to women. There is a big variation in the numbers and proportions of men and women employed in each arm or service. Women constitute a very small proportion of the RA (4.8 per cent), the Royal Electrical and Mechanical Engineers (REME) (3 per cent) and the Royal Engineers (1.1 per cent). These are the three areas in which posts were opened up to women in 1998. In 2006, the RA, REME and the RE were 7,860, 11,300 and 10,300 strong respectively, and had 380, 340 and 110 women respectively. In arms or services where women have a longer tradition of employment – in the combat service support functions – women are present in much greater numbers and constitute a higher proportion of service strength. In 2006, women constituted 17.2 per cent of the personnel in the Intelligence Corps (270 female personnel) and over one-quarter of the Adjutant General's Corps (29.5 per cent, over 2,000 female personnel) and of the Royal Army Medical Corps (28.3 per cent, just over 900 female personnel). They constituted 11 per cent of the Royal Logistics Corps (1,890 women) and 10.2 per cent of the Royal Signals (940 women).

There are three points to note about the patterns shown by these statistics. The first is that patterns of female employment in the Army broadly follow the gender division of labour in civilian sectors, where the distribution and proportions of men and women vary widely across different sectors (primary extractive, manufacturing, service occupations and so on) and across different occupational classifications (skilled manual, clerical and administrative, managerial roles, professional occupations). In the civilian labour market, there has been a trend over the past 50 years for an overall increase in levels of female engagement in waged labour outside the home. Women's engagement in the labour market has been concentrated in service sector occupations, particularly in health and education, and in the services and retail sectors. The patterns of women's employment in the Army therefore mirror those in the civilian labour market.

The second point to note is that, although official Ministry of Defence and Army statements on the deployment of women personnel usually highlight an upwards trend in both proportions and overall numbers of women in the Army, annual increases are very small. The idea that the British Army of the early twenty-first century has been over-run with women, feminised even, is hard to support.[80] Indeed, in some arms and services, the data on the numbers of senior women personnel is skewed because of the rounding used, which distorts what are actually very small figures.

Third, statistics on the distribution of all personnel across different functions within the Army show quite clearly the significance of the infantry to that Army. Ongoing debates, whether internal to the Army at elite policy levels or in populist commentary, wrestle with the wider issues raised around the use of infantry, and these are arguments that spring from a variety of positions. For some, in the modern, technologically driven Army the need for boots on the ground is less important, and this argument spills over into debates about the future gendered make-up of an Army increasingly driven by needs to man equipment rather than equipping the man. It is easy, in an era celebratory of techno-efficiency, to be seduced by arguments emphasising the utility of precision armaments in removing the need for ground-based forces. Yet, as Lewis Page persuasively argues, the infantry remains indispensable as the controllable and thus variable element of force, a pre-requisite of all military operations because of the versatility of infantry troops in providing not only close combat direct engagement, but also other constabulary functions as well.[81] We return to this in the concluding chapter, but raise it here to emphasise that arguments around women and men's military participation always circulate with reference to wider discourses around the deployment of military power.

As Mady Wechsler Segal has emphasised, there is a circularity to patterns of participation that we should recognise as more significant to the overall story.[82] The MoD narrative, presented on its website, emphasises a linear narrative of incremental progress: 'Today, the contribution of Servicewomen to the combat effectiveness of the Armed Forces is essential. More women are serving in a greater variety of posts than ever before, many of them front line.'[83]

The narrative around the Imperial War Museum's major exhibition on women and war echoed the same idea of persistent progress, and the title of the book that accompanied the exhibition, *From Corsets to Camouflage*, echoes this with the idea of escape from female confinement and the emancipation of anonymity. Such linear narratives obscure the circularities and the similarities in patterns around women's participation.

In understanding these patterns, we also want to draw attention to the limits of observations based on statistical data, such as that which we deploy (at a very simple level) here. The data presented here show clearly that the numbers of women employed in the Army, although gradually increasing, remain small, and that men dominate across all arms and services (totally, in the case of the infantry). The statistics also show clearly that proportions are markedly different in different arms and services. What the statistics cannot explain is the lived experience of men and women, as gendered beings, within these different arms and sectors. Statistics are only a starting point in understanding gender dynamics. The gender culture needs explaining and to do this we have to draw on other types of data and sources of information. Furthermore, given a historical pattern evident in the gendered history of the Army, of the containment of women's military participation, the question that follows is whether this pattern of containment persists and how it operates. This question is addressed in Chapter 3.

3 British Army personnel policies and the politics of female difference

This chapter looks at female difference and how this is understood within Army policy and within its gendered culture. Public and media-based discussion, academic inquiry and Army policy itself all recognise that men and women are different, often in narratives that suggest that the act of identifying that difference is merely an act of stating the obvious and sufficient to explain the gender politics of this institution. We are interested in taking this observation further. If men and women are different, how is that difference understood within the Army? How does male and female difference shape gender relations and gender identities for men and women personnel? If, as is commonly believed, the Army is a sexist institution in that it prioritises or favours one group (male) over another (female), how are such practices supported and sustained?

In Chapter 2, we set out a gendered history of the Army, and argued that in order to understand men and women's different levels of participation and modes of engagement within the Army we need to recognise the ways in which female participation is contained. We noted the expression of this containment in the uneven distribution of women across the different arms and services within the contemporary Army. In this chapter we look at how that containment works through a politics of difference. We examine a number of different policies aimed explicitly or implicitly at women's military participation. These are policies on the opening up of posts to women from 1998 onwards, gender issues around policies on recruit selection and training, the evolution of equal opportunities and diversity policies, and the policies around the exclusion of women from direct combat posts. What we are interested in is not an evaluation of these initiatives *per se* in terms of the advancement of women's participation in the Army, but rather an understanding of how ideas about gender and difference are constructed and reproduced at a policy level. We then go on to look at how these ideas of female difference shape gender relations by looking at the results of recent MoD-sponsored research into sexual harassment. This research suggests that despite attempts at a policy level to promote a culture of equality and respect for difference within the Army, a wider culture exists, which is hostile to female differences from male norms. Our argument is not just that the contemporary British Army sees men and women as different in their capacity as soldiers, but that the ways in which male/female difference is explained has wider ramifications for the extent to which women can be fully included within this fighting force.

These are not the only areas of policy intervention around gender, directly or indirectly, within the British Army (and indeed the armed forces). Another significant area is the policies structuring the connections between work, home, family life and parenthood for personnel, particularly the care of dependents of men and women posted on operations at short notice, and the raft of policies and formal support networks directed at the needs of the spouses of the Army (usually, but not exclusively, wives). The needs of Army spouses have always been recognised as a military issue because of the importance of family and spousal support for the morale of serving soldiers and the retention of trained personnel.[1] We have chosen these policy areas because they speak to issues central to the construction of female difference through military performance.

Discourse, organisations and policy

In this and subsequent chapters, we talk a lot about discourses. Discourses are systems of ideas or concepts through which things are given meaning.[2] These things that are made meaningful through discourse may be material entities or social practices. Discourses are social phenomena, in that they are created and sustained by people, through social interaction and communication. Discourses are representational activities. It follows from this that discourses are fluid, in that they are constantly being developed and shaped by processes of articulation, reproduction and circulation, in order to give meaning to things. They are also specific to time and space – the discourses that circulate around women in the contemporary British Army are distinct to that time and place – although there will be historical continuities, there will also be ruptures, and although there will be similarities between militaries, these will be contingent on the specificities of situation. Discourses may be dominant or contested, or somewhere in between; whatever the case they are political in that they shape practice and construct explanations around those practices which promote particular interpretations of the world and deny or silence other views. The key idea around which this chapter is framed is that discourses of gender in the Army need to be identified, examined and understood if we are to fully understand how the politics of gender play out within that institution. In this chapter, we look primarily at policy documentation and debates as a location for discursive constructions of gender, and argue that through a reading of these we can identify the discourses that represent women in specific ways.

Policy, by which we mean institutional frameworks for doing things, may seem initially an offbeat topic for scrutiny using the methods of discourse analysis.[3] Policies set out what is to be done to address an issue. But policies are more than that. In order to address an issue, policies have to be based on an understanding of that issue, and most usually policies that 'do things' are devised because there are recognised problems or difficulties around the issue in question. Policies, then, frame issues around identifiable problems, and by so doing they construct issues as problems. A first step in this type of policy analysis, then, is to be alert to the ways in which a problem is constructed, how an issue is made into a problem. A second step is to see what the policy actually does; what changes does a specific policy or group of policies aim to achieve? A third step reviews the wider implications of strategies for change; what assumptions about the world and the way it works frame the mechanisms for implementation?

Viewed in this way, policy analysis becomes less an evaluation exercise, of assessing the goodness-of-fit between suggested changes and the issue to which they are addressed, and becomes instead an exercise in exploring how issues are constructed within their context. Policy documents, and the institutional practices that are implicated in their formation, provide a source of information on an institution's ideas. Discourses that circulate within policy give an institutional view to compare and contrast with the subjectivities and specificities of lived experience and personal practice.

In this chapter, we are concerned with policies developed within the Ministry of Defence (MoD) and the British Army, related institutions that plan for and implement the government's political objectives where this requires the use or threat of lethal force. Further observations follow from this. When talking about 'military policy' we are referring to a vast and diverse range of orders, directives, frameworks and strategies on everything from the supply of food to orders of battle. We deal with policies relating to men and women's military participation, a very small part of the policy frameworks that facilitate the existence and operational capability of the armed forces. We deal with policies that have been developed at an elite level by the MoD and the Army's directorates with responsibility for personnel issues, but which also have direct input from bodies such as parliament, through the defence committees of both Houses. Personnel policies, broadly defined, are also an area of interest to the government's statutory advisers on equality issues, primarily the Equal Opportunities Commission (EOC) and the Commission for Racial Equality (CRE). In an analysis of policy discourses, we see how issues are constructed both within the military as an institution, but also as a practice in which civilian and military institutions work collaboratively or in opposition to define the meaning of things.

The expansion of posts available to women soldiers

The first policy issue that we consider is the expansion of employment options open to women soldiers, which came into effect on 1 April 1998. As we saw in Chapter 2, following the major defence review under the *Options for Change* White Paper, separate women's units in the Army, Navy and Royal Air Force were disbanded in 1992. Following the disbanding of the Women's Royal Army Corps (WRAC), the majority of personnel were incorporated into the newly formed Adjutant General's Corps, but other options primarily in logistics, signals and medical services became open to women as well. As the statistics in Chapter 2 show, the uneven distribution of women across the Army reflects these patterns of redeployment, over a decade later.

The expansion of posts was announced in Parliament on 27 October 1997 by the then Secretary of State for Defence. Posts in hitherto male-only corps would from 1 April 1998 be open to both men and women. These were posts in the Royal Artillery, the Royal Engineers and the Royal Electrical and Mechanical Engineers.[4] Posts in the Infantry, the Household Cavalry, the Royal Marines and the RAF Regiment were exempt, and were to remain closed to women on the grounds that these were direct combat positions. (We discuss this issue below.) The proportion of posts open to women in the Army thus increased from 47 per cent to 70 per cent. This is the still the situation as we write.

This policy change was framed for public consumption around two ideas. The first was of a modern and socially engaged armed forces: "If we are to properly modernise our Armed Forces, we must also bring our personnel policies up to date. The Armed Forces must represent the society they defend if they are not to become isolated from it.'[5]

A second idea established as a basis for this change a business case for equality of opportunity, framing the shift as a requirement of the institution, rather than as a response to wider social or feminist pressure or demands from men and women within the armed forces: 'We want to see Armed Forces which truly reflect our increasingly multi-cultural society and one in which women as well as men have every opportunity to progress. We also want the very best of our youth in the forces and if there are artificial barriers to recruiting the best, whether it be from among the ethnic minorities or among women, then our pool of excellence is diminished as a result.'[6]

The expansion in posts open to women was equated with modernity, progress, gender equity and the benefits brought to the institution by a diverse workforce. In terms of the representations of gender implicated in statements surrounding the policy change, women were presented as equal to men as valued and capable members of the armed forces.[7] Although silent on the idea that political equity agendas external to the armed forces had forced this change, a press release issued eleven months after the policy change came into effect tied the expansion of opportunities for women securely to a feminist agenda:

> New figures released today by the Ministry of Defence reveal that every day is International Women's Day in the Armed Forces with Servicewomen deployed around the world defending the nation's interests . . . Armed Forces Minister Doug Henderson welcomed the latest figures: . . . 'This is a welcome trend and a positive affirmation of our policies – making sure that every day is an international women's day in the modern Armed Forces. Women are reaching the most senior ranks – Army Brigadiers, Navy Captains and Commodores, and RAF Air Commodores. The Services only promote the brightest and best regardless of gender, and very few organisations can boast the recruitment of women to one in every five management posts.'[8]

As we indicated in Chapter 2, a further explanation of the expansion of posts revolves around necessity. Writing on the basis of research conducted on behalf of the MoD, Christopher Dandeker and Fiona Paton note the recruitment crisis besetting the three services from the beginning of the 1990s onwards, ironic in view of the 30 per cent cut in manning levels brought about by *Options for Change*. Demographic changes including a fall in the overall numbers of teenagers within the potential recruitment pool, economic changes including the buoyancy of the British economy and the consequent strength of the civilian labour market at the time, and changes in social attitudes (characterised as a 'post-deferential society') making the discipline and structure of the armed forces less and less attractive to school-leavers could also be seen as explanatory factors for the opening of posts to women at this time.[9] Quite simply, the armed forces were fishing for recruits in a shrinking pool of available fit, willing, suitable young male labour, its more traditional recruits. Strategies representing women as equally valued members of the Army team therefore had an element of necessity to them.

It is instructive, writing eight years after the expansion of posts, to look at the statistical data for women's participation in the arms or services that became open to them in 1998. In 1998, 3.8 per cent of the Royal Artillery (330 personnel) were women. In 2006, this figure was 4.8 per cent (380 women), a decline from a peak of 5.7 per cent (500 women) in 2000. In the Royal Engineers, in 1998 a mere 10 women constituted 0.1 per cent of its trained strength, rising to 380 women (4.8 per cent) in 2006, its highest level. In the Royal Electrical and Mechanical Engineers, 2.3 per cent of the trained strength were women (260 personnel), rising to 3.0 per cent (340 women) by 2006, again its highest level.[10] Clearly, although the expansion of posts has enabled some women to participate in artillery, combat engineering and mechanical engineering trades, these posts are of limited appeal to the majority of Army women.

Policy discourse is silent on the explanations for the gendered division of labour within the armed forces. As we discussed in Chapter 2, a cursory glance of this structuring of the military labour market shows that it follows patterns long evident in the wider civilian labour market. Writing a decade ago, Christopher Dandeker and Mady Wechsler Segal predicted that some arms and services would continue to be the ones in which men constituted the overwhelming majority, whereas others would accommodate a much higher proportion of women.[11] We should emphasise, however, that the nature of the work alone does not appear to affect gender representation; other factors such as the context for the integration of individual occupations will be significant, and in occupations newly opened to women, as Margaret Harrell and colleagues observe, the experiences and performance and participation of pioneer women in newly integrated military occupations may not be representative because of pioneer effects.[12] The factors that influence women's decisions to join (and to remain in or leave) particular occupations (and the military more generally) are varied and include recruitment strategies, training and physical selection processes and standards, career progression opportunities, clothing and equipment issues, the existence or lack of family-friendly practices, sexual and gender harassment, whether a critical mass of women exists, attitudes and perceptions about military careers, and leadership commitments.[13]

To these ideas we can add those that our research interviewees – men and women with responsibility for gender issues in various ways in various branches of the Army – themselves drew on to make sense of the gender division of labour within the Army. One idea was that women who join the armed forces are consciously self-selecting, choosing careers and posts with which they feel they will have the greatest chance of acceptance because of cultures of military practice, perceived to vary in their degree of hostility or acceptance of women across the Army. Another was that the type of woman attracted to an Army career in the first place was likely to be motivated by demands for a more intellectually stimulating job than those perceived to be found in combat arms – hence the high proportion of women in intelligence functions, for example. A further idea is that, despite the physical screening process at selection (which we discuss in more detail below), the physical demands of certain posts, particularly in engineering and artillery, are recognised by many women recruits as essentially beyond their physical capabilities. These contrasting commentaries on women's uneven participation, despite the expansion of posts, are indicative of the complexities inherent in explaining women's and men's differential rates of military participation. So, although official policy discourse at the time of the post expansion was boosterist about women's employability and across the Army, and was emphatic about the progressiveness that the expansion was indicative of, this policy discourse has to be understood in the context of other discourses around women's potential as soldiers, influential to women recruits and soldiers as well as within policy circles.

Selection and training

The second policy area we have chosen for discussion is Army selection and training. In 1998, concurrent with the expansion of posts open to women, the Army introduced a new scheme for the assessment of the physical capabilities of potential recruits. Physical Selection Standards (Recruits) [PSS(R)] is one of a number of tests of ability, aptitude and potential carried out on potential recruits at recruit selection centres during the two-day selection process, attended by those who have passed an initial screening process for joining the Army.

PSS(R) had its origins externally and much of the pressure on the Army to introduce these new selection standards came from the EOC. The EOC had long argued that having different physical selection tests for men and women applicants to the Army was discriminatory. It was directly discriminatory against men who passed the lower standard required of women but were denied access to jobs in the Armed Forces. But having the same fitness standards for men and women could indirectly discriminate against women who pass the tests in much smaller proportions. The tests were devised, therefore, against job-related criteria; on the basis of an analysis of all the posts in the Army, the physical fitness standards required for each post were identified. These new tests were designed to provide a scientifically based assessment of an individual's suitability for their intended career employment group, and to predict how an individuals' performance could improve during training under the Common Military Syllabus (Recruits) [CMS(R)]. The tests include a 1.5-mile (c. 2.5-km) run, single lift and carrying tests, sit-ups and a loaded march, and each test has five pass levels. Access to every post in the Army is dependent on the level of performance. The tests were designed and publicised as 'gender free', and tied to the Army's declared objectives of widening the range of career options open to women soldiers.

These tests were portrayed as innovative and scientifically immutable, a means by which sex-derived physical difference could be controlled for through the application of modern scientific rationality: 'The introduction of PSS(R) . . . will take the army to the forefront of physiological research, providing us with a selection protocol which is truly gender free and legally defensible. Furthermore, it enhances the Army's reputation as a forward-looking, non-discriminatory employer which takes seriously the duty of care it has for its recruits.'[14]

Through controlling for physical sex-based difference, it was possible to present these tests as 'gender free', not through the dismissal of male and female difference but through a mechanism for accounting for that difference. In the words of one defence commentator, the new tests could 'cope with women entrants who have different skills to men. Women, for example, do not have as much upper body strength and are commonly better shots on the range where they have skill and accuracy not shown by men'.[15]

In controlling for gender difference, the tests were presented as a mechanism for opening up opportunities for both men and women in the Army, matching an individual's strength and skills to different military tasks and roles. In addition, for some commentators, the introduction of the tests supported arguments that predicted the declining significance of physical ability and strength in modern armed forces and the corresponding increase in the significance of technological proficiency amongst personnel in order to operate the increasingly sophisticated equipment used in modern modes of warfare.

The introduction of PSS(R) was latched on to by commentaries using this as a vehicle for expressing wider anxieties about a perceived decline in male physicality. One cartoon that appeared in 1998 in the *Daily Express* (26 August 1997) depicted a sergeant major instructing his corporal to wake a new recruit gently with a cup of tea, an expression of the unease about what the new selection process might bring to a military regime viewed as necessarily tough on raw recruits. Another, published in *The Independent* on 25 August 1997, depicted a physical training instructor embodied in stance as barrel-chested and straight-backed yet dressed as an aerobics teacher and wiggling his bottom, instructing his class to wait for the beat of the music blaring from a cassette player, again an expression of unease about what were constructed as feminised fitness practices being imported into this male world. The idea that the new tests were somehow compensatory for declining standards amongst male recruits proved hard to shake. Our own interviews with people with experience of recruitment, selection and training produced evidence of a concern that the lifestyles and backgrounds of recruits were progressively more and more at odds with the physical and personal traits necessary for the Army.[16] The defence commentator and historian Anthony Beevor had observed that during the late 1980s a discernible difference in the calibre and outlook of recruits was emerging, identifiable, for example, in the unrealistic expectations amongst young recruits about the benefits that would automatically flow to them as a result of military participation.[17] Official MoD comment on the introduction of the new tests, although dismissive of the idea that the tests were somehow indicative that the British Army had gone soft in response to the changing quality of recruits, nonetheless supported the argument that shifts in the calibre of potential recruits (particularly lower basic fitness levels) required a revised approach in both selection and training:

> This approach is about modernising, not mollycoddling. It is not about turning sergeants into social workers, it is about turning today's young recruits into professional soldiers. It is about facing up to the challenges of a changed society and doing something about it rather than merely standing on the sidelines while our Army gets more and more under strength and our soldiers get more and more overstretched. To do that would be a real betrayal of our Army, our country and our young people.[18]

The integrated training of men and women under CMS(R) was not without problems. Specifically, evaluations of the progress of recruits showed that integrated training brought much higher levels of injury and rates of medical discharge for female recruits than for male. So although the PSS(R) process ensured that individual recruits were tested against job-related rather than arbitrary criteria, and matched against the future demands of their role in the Army, the introduction of gender-free training was identified as leading to the increase in female injury and medical discharge rates.[19] In an assessment of possible procedures for streaming recruits to reduce injuries, the Army Training and Recruiting Agency was keen to dispel what it termed the myth that equal opportunities legislation was a root cause of the problem. It concluded that the equal opportunities legislation did not dictate that men and women would have to progress through the same training syllabus at the same rate.[20] It recommended that, following gender-free selection, training should be single sex, so that women's fitness could be developed at a pace commensurate with their physiology, a practice long in place in British Army officer training. This move was also recommended in the Adult Learning Inspectorate (ALI)'s report on safer training, a move this organisation constructed as the abandonment of a gender-free approach to training women to one that was 'gender fair'.[21]

The move to single-sex training indicates a recognition – and acceptance – of female physical difference. The paper which outlined the rationale for the move and recommended the shift to gender streaming termed this a change from 'train hard, fight easy' to 'train smart, fight easy', mirroring accepted practice amongst athletes and enabled by the advances in physiological research and data measurement. It followed that 'individual differences only become problematic if they are not catered for accordingly'.[22] It will be interesting to see how the shift to single-sex training proceeds and whether this will be unproblematic for women trainees or otherwise. The ALI were explicit about the cultures that revolved around physical ability: 'A culture which values physical strength arguably finds it difficult to find a place for women appropriate to their potential contribution, and exalts "hardness" in a manner which can promote bullying'.[23] Whether this will feed problems with the acceptance of women trained under the single-sex regime, or the new regime will be judged on its own merits, is open to question at the time of writing.

Equal opportunities and diversity

Our third area for discussion is policies on equal opportunities and diversity management, policies that speak directly but not exclusively into debates on women's military participation. Here, as before, we are interested both in the introduction of measures to deal with issues surrounding equality of opportunity, and also in the language and discourses through which these measures were introduced, justified and explained to audiences both inside and outside the British Army. We argue that the shift towards the framing of gender equity policy as a diversity management issue is indicative about the construction of ideas of gender and female differences within this institution.

The roots of the contemporary British Army's equal opportunities and diversity strategies lie in concerns expressed through the British CRE, following public revelations to the CRE and through the print and broadcast media about high levels of racism and racist harassment in the Army, given public profile from the mid-1980s onwards.[24] The Equal Opportunities Action Plan that emerged in response was not prompted by concerns about gender equity, but it did address harassment and unfair treatment as issues faced both by women and by members of minority ethnic groups. In addition, the EOC had had (and still has) a role in supporting individual complains about unequal treatment in the armed forces, bought by members against the MoD.[25]

The 1998 Strategic Defence Review consolidated equality of opportunity as an explicit objective within personnel policies, and initiated a strategy, the Armed Forces Overarching Personnel Strategy (AFOPS) within which equity issues were framed and codified. The 1999 White Paper provides a good example of the MoD argument about equal opportunities and its obligations with regard to the equitable treatment of its military employees:

> The Armed Forces place the highest priority on equal opportunities . . . Our aim is to achieve universal acceptance and application of a working environment free from harassment, intimidation and unlawful discrimination in which all have equal opportunity based on merit, consistent with our legal obligation, to realise their potential in contributing to the maintenance and enhancement of operational effectiveness.[26]

The language of the AFOPS and of the Chief of the General Staff's 2000 Equal Opportunities Directive repeats this view, that equality of opportunity is about both equity in treatment and freedom from abuse and that this should be seen within the context of operational requirements.

One outcome of the AFOPS was the introduction of training in equity issues amongst staff. This was implemented through the training of officers of the rank of brigadier (or equivalent) and above through a one-day training programme in equal opportunities awareness, and with the training of those who, in turn, held responsibility for equal opportunities issues at unit level. This was conducted through the Tri-Service Equal Opportunities Training Centre (TSEOTC), later to be renamed the Joint Equality and Diversity Training Centre (JEDTC). Awareness about equity issues was also disseminated through the training process, both at basic training level and in higher-level courses leading to promotion. The emphasis in much of this training was on equal opportunities measures as mechanisms to limit abuse, both racist and sexist in nature. For example, one of the Army's Individual Training Directives [ITD(A) 10],[27] notes that a key outcome of AFOPS is the introduction of training in equity issues amongst staff.

> The Army is fully committed to Equal Opportunities and to providing a working environment free from discrimination and harassment as well as equality of opportunity for all Army personnel within the framework of the law, irrespective of sex, marital status, race, ethnic origin or religious belief. Army policy is crystal clear – discrimination and harassment of any kind is not to be tolerated.[28]

Pamphlets such as *Values and Standards in the British Army* were distributed to serving soldiers, and such publications set out an argument about equal opportunities in a similar vein, establishing it as a 'zero tolerance' issue.

The Army's deployment of an equal opportunities strategy, then, rested initially on a strategy of downwards dissemination through the chain of command of an understanding of equal opportunities as an issue affecting people's abilities to do their jobs. In a culture that is often stereotyped as valuing aggression and having an ability to transcend harsh treatment, the emphasis on equality as a fairness and an operational issue is unsurprising, a deliberate choice of framing amongst many for an environment culturally hostile to many civilian (and feminist) discourses around equality and rights. A flavour of this is given in a quotation from the *Values and Standards* pamphlet, which says that equal opportunities is not about 'pretending everyone is the same, giving advantage to certain groups, lowering standards or setting quotas'.[29] The equal opportunities strategies of the late 1990s were also a presentational strategy, by which we mean that much emphasis was placed on communicating initiatives such as equal opportunities training to a wider civilian public in order to counter public concerns about discriminatory treatment within the armed forces, and to promote the idea of an armed forces getting its house in order in response to criticism. Given the ongoing recruitment crisis through the 1990s, this is a rational strategy by an employer conscious of its public image in a competitive labour market.

Most significantly, the statements around equal opportunities at this time are explicit in the framing of equity issues within discourses of operational effectiveness. What is notable is less the fact of this connection; this is an argument that we would expect the Army to make. It is interesting because of the extents to which this argument is made to hold. What is interesting – and we go into this below – is the way that female difference becomes the central idea through which the issue of operational effectiveness is argued.

Around 1999, there is a shift in the language of employment equity in statements by the Army, traceable in policy documentation. The talk becomes less of the provision of equal opportunities for all, and more of the management of a diverse workforce. The idea of equity as a diversity management issue emerges in the 1990s, initially in the private sector but extending to government agencies and networking organisations.[30] So we see both in the 1999 Defence White Paper and in the 2000 AFOPS the use of the language of diversity: 'We must recruit and retain the best people for the job from a diverse society', for example.[31] This shift in the Army was sealed with a name change in 2001, when the Equal Opportunities Action Plan because the Diversity Action Plan 2001–5, by-lined 'from EO into diversity'. The Tri-Service Equal Opportunities Training Centre (TSEOTC) newsletter to equal opportunities advisers at unit level became an *Equality and Diversity* publication, and the Army and MoD websites started using the two terms together.

This shift is language was indicative of deeper conceptual change. As one Army spokesperson explained it, the shift to diversity presupposes that a legal framework for compliance for equal opportunities responsibilities is already in place through its codification in rules. Diversity takes a next step and allows for the management of equity while also explicitly recognising difference. This was presented to us in research interviews with Army officers as an evolutionary rather than revolutionary change: differences between men and women could be recognised, and worked with. This idea had its roots in 1997 guidelines on the employment of women, who were to be recognised as 'not the same as men: they are neither better nor worse, they are different.'[32] By 2002, the language around diversity was fully deployed in Army communications:

> Army EO policy lists those minorities whom CGS says you must not treat unfairly. Diversity policy says that if you treat all your people fairly and with respect, they will work harder. It recognises differences in people's abilities and needs, but believes that the sum of those abilities improves the performance of teams. That makes it more than worthwhile to work on overcoming individual weaknesses.[33]

In remarking on the shift to diversity, the difference was highlighted between the codification of rules to bring about equity and a diversity management approach, presented as being more flexible in its ability to deal with inequities and less adversarial:

> EO policy says that some minorities have equal rights i.e. to education, training and jobs etc. Diversity policy would say that notwithstanding those rights, all people have different needs; dealing with these makes the individual more

> productive. EO policy gives minorities an opportunity to challenge inequality through the courts. Diversity policy is a management ethos which recognises inequality and tackles it wherever it occurs.[34]

Diversity management, then, was presented as a much more wide-reaching human resource strategy, in comparison to the rigidities of equal opportunities compliance.

A number of ideas can be read off from the shift to the management of diversity in the policies surrounding equity issues. The first is that the promotion of equity issues under the banner of diversity management is part of strategy for changing public perceptions of the attractiveness of the Army as a career of choice for able, suitably qualified young people. At a time when the civilian labour market was buoyant and the competition for suitably qualified recruits was intense because of this, it provided a way for the Army to rebadge itself. Diversity management promotes the idea of the Army as an attractive employer to an increasingly multi-ethnic social base, suspicious of the Army's abilities and willingness to deal with racism in the ranks, and brought up with expectations of parity and equity in employment for both men and women. The Ministry of Defence was quite explicit in making a business case for the shift to the management of diversity. For example, the 1999 Defence White Paper noted that:

> The Armed Forces need to recruit, promote and retain the highest quality personnel. They need, therefore, to recruit from the widest pool of talent, which includes personnel of different race, ethnic origin, religion, gender or social background. The Services require a demanding mix of skills and experience; individuals can provide these irrespective of their ethnic background or gender.[35]

Diversity management was therefore about attracting diversity of talent: 'The eradication of discrimination, harassment and intimidation, and the provision of genuine equality of opportunity, creates the conditions for the Army to recruit and retain the very best quality of officers and soldiers, and to make the most of their diverse talents and abilities.'[36] The business case was explicit, diversity management being portrayed as 'recruiting more people who meet our standards. Retaining more people with the right qualities, and therefore getting a better return on our investment'.[37] The shift to diversity management, then, is a business strategy.

The second point about the shift to diversity is the establishment of a moral basis for this shift, in contrast with the legal basis provided by equal opportunities legislation. This was presented explicitly as a shift that accorded and fitted with the moral codes, values and standards of the British Army. In a newsletter to equal opportunities trainers and advisers, this correspondence was made explicit: 'to our civilian friends, Diversity is a new and delicious wine in smart bottles; to us it is a rather fine vintage that we have always had in the cellar but sometimes forget to drink.'[38]

For example, the personnel management requirements indicated under diversity management strategies were explained as corresponding to existing practice within the Army, particularly regimes of training aimed at drawing out and consolidating an individual's strengths:

> This requires each person to be managed individually for his or her personal needs. The style of management respects the individual and ensures that they are treated fairly and with dignity. All these 'new' ideas should already be covered under good robust leadership and the military ethos. We would therefore like to make the link that diversity is not a marginal policy for women and ethnic minorities, but the translation of the best practices of leadership and the military ethos.[39]

By eliding new shifts in the emphasis of equity policies with existing Army practices, the shift to diversity becomes less stark:

> [I]f you think of the military ethos, and define what the ethos is, what are the constituent parts of that ethos? You think about commitment, loyalty, respect for others, discipline, self-discipline, a moral integrity and so on, these things sit absolutely within the context of what equality and diversity is all about, which is treating people fairly.[40]

The 'military ethos' to which this interviewee referred is codified in documentation that sets out for soldiers and commander what the values and standards of the British Army are. Qualities include selfless commitment, courage, discipline, integrity, loyalty and respect for others, and there is explicit emphasis on the duty of an individual to assess the impacts of their actions on operational effectiveness. Personnel are expected to adhere to the law, and to contribute towards an environment free from bullying, harassment and discrimination.[41] As we say elsewhere,

> By wrapping up the respectful treatment of others in a codified set of standards about behaviour, 'demonstrating fair play, by ensuring that everyone is treated with respect', the management of diversity is presented as a reflection of wider Army practice, which in turn is portrayed as providing the conditions under which all members of a team are able to contribute to towards the wider objectives of the Army.[42]

The final point to make about the shift to diversity management is what it means in terms of discourses of gender circulating within the Army. This was a shift made in good faith by those responsible for equity policies in the belief that the emphasis on diversity was both appropriate and progressive. In pointing out the political consequences of this discursive shift, we are not criticising directly the motivations that prompted this shift. What we *are* doing, however, is pointing out the conceptual issues this raises for understandings of gender in the contemporary British Army.

Discourses of diversity obscure power and structural inequalities; all differences are equated, whatever their basis or origin. The emphasis on diversity removes consideration of power differences and minimises discussion of the sources of disadvantage. The social origins of difference are underplayed; as one commentator has noted, diversity management strategies can be interpreted as 'a good looking cover for inaction'.[43] The use of the language of diversity makes equity issues more palatable to some than the more directly political language of equality of opportunity with its basis in legal frameworks and legal obligations. This has been strategically beneficial for the Army, as it allows the presentation of equity issues within a framework that makes them distant from ideas about 'political correctness'. The framing of equity policies as political correctness – and the difficulties that ensue because of this – was highlighted by a number of our interviewees, and a 2005 report by the ALI on safer training made this point also; a culture of antipathy towards equity issues within the Army has in large part drawn strength from the ability of reluctant soldiers to draw on a discourse that circulates extensively within popular culture (particularly the print media), which constructs equity strategies aimed at the resolution of the legitimate grievances of a minority as an irrational practice. This discourse is identifiable, for example, in the phrase 'political correctness gone mad'. But a by-product of the shift to diversity is the way that the emphasis on the management of difference shifts all attention away from the fact that the construction of difference is itself a social practice, rooted in unequal power relations and discriminatory practice. We concur with Victoria Basham's argument that all differences (between men and women, between different ethnic groups, and so on) are social in origin; the process of defining difference is a social practice.[44] Difference then becomes assumed as a given, rather than the outcome of social practices in which we are all complicit. The emphasis on the management of that difference underscores this; the social origins of difference are ignored, it becomes impossible to speak of these.

Furthermore, the emphasis on the diversity of all soldiers means that gender can be downgraded as an axis of difference. In some ways this is a positive move, in that markers of female difference, such as physical differences, can be sidelined as a point of identification. Indeed, PSS(R) and single-sex training does this by recognising the physiological differences between men and women, dealing with these through a system of assessment that matches recruits to jobs, and thus overcoming these differences. However, there are limits to this; some differences cannot be overcome when compared with a male norm. We would argue that where these differences cannot be overcome, female difference is constructed as problematic on the basis of its visibility. In the words of one of our interviewees: '[A]t the end of the day, we know that a bloke's a bloke and a woman's a woman and actually there's a much greater difference between men and women . . . than there is between somebody who's white and somebody who's black.'[45]

And, to conclude, what of equity policies in the contemporary British Army? Despite the establishment of clear policy guidelines clarifying the need for all soldiers to refrain from abusive and discriminatory behaviour, and despite the rebadging of equity issues as diversity management issues, there is substantial evidence that a culture remains in the Army that can be antipathetic to women's participation and to the participation of visible minority groups. The ALI report of 2005 offered a stinging rebuke to those who considered these issues satisfactorily dealt with, noting that equal opportunities was 'a critical area for rapid improvement'.[46] The report noted that, although there was public commitment, the framing of equal opportunities as the outcome of 'political correctness' persisted. Despite public claims to the contrary, some Army establishments failed to comply even with basic service requirements regarding the treatment of others. Although all recruits received briefings about and training around equal opportunities issues, there was a big variation in the quality of that training. The misapprehension that equal opportunities was about treating all people the same (despite the arguments of ITD(A) 10 to the contrary) persisted.[47]

Combat exclusion, operational effectiveness and gender

The fourth area of policy debate to be considered is one which cuts to the heart of arguments about women's military participation and the construction of female difference in policy discourse; the exclusion of women from direct combat posts. Although the Army might advertise itself as an equal opportunities employer, under section 85(4) of the 1995 Sex Discrimination Act, amended by the 2006 Equality Act, British Armed Forces are exempt in respect of 'an act done for the purpose of ensuring the combat effectiveness of naval, military and air forces of the Crown'. And although in practice women are often drawn into direct combat roles, official policy is that direct combat units are male only. Combat posts are defined as those where personnel are required to close with and kill the enemy using direct fire weapons.

The exclusion of women from combat positions is an area of ongoing policy debate. The British EOC have argued consistently that posts in the Army should be open to all on the basis of ability, and not closed to some of the basis of sex.[48] With the opening up of new jobs to women in 1998 came an announcement to Parliament that the issue of women's combat exclusion would be considered in detail within the MoD.[49] This study was a long time coming; it was not until May 2002 that the report on *The Employment of Women in the Armed Forces* was published. The report concluded that women would not be permitted to join direct combat units, because of the risks this participation was seen to pose to operational effectiveness. Operational effectiveness could potentially be undermined because the presence of women could have a negative impact on unit cohesion.

> Under the conditions of high intensity, close-quarter battle, group cohesion becomes of much greater significance to team performance and, in such an environment, failure can have far-reaching and grave consequences. To admit women therefore, would involve a risk without any offsetting gains in terms of combat effectiveness.[50]

Women, according to the line of argument presented in the report, constituted a risk to team performance under the stress of close quarter combat:

> The key point is that in battle, each individual in a team, while under extreme pressure including pervasive uncertainty and imminent fear of death, must summon up the continuing determination to go forward with an absolute focus and impose their will on the enemy. They must then go on to do so again and again over a period of days or even weeks. Even the smallest failure at this level can affect adjoining teams and thus spread to threaten the objectives of the larger unit.[51]

The risks posed by the inclusion of women were not, however, explained on the basis of differences of physical ability. Indeed, the report was quite clear, following its review of the literature and of field-based exercises, that some soldiers with the requisite physical strength would meet the required standards of physiological capability to cope with the extreme demands of close quarter battle, regardless of their sex. Furthermore, despite male and female differences in levels of aggression, some women would be able to summon the required levels of controlled aggression seen as necessary for direct combat engagements. Rather, the issue was presented as revolving around unit or group cohesion. Ultimately, the decision was presented as resting on the deployment of a precautionary principle:

> We have no way of knowing whether mixed gender teams can develop the bonds of unconditional trust, loyalty and mutual support that must be strong enough to survive the test of close combat. Nor can we tell what will be the impact on the other members of a team if a member of the opposite sex is killed or maimed. Moreover, there is no way of testing to find out, since no conceivable trial could simulate the full effects of close combat.[52]

The policy justifying women's exclusion or exemption from direct combat posts rested therefore on supposition and doubt (fear, even) about the effect that they would have on the ability of fighting teams to undertake direct combat missions.

The idea of unit cohesion presented in the report constructs it as automatically and inherently operationally beneficial. No commentator, within or outwith the Army, would doubt the significance of unit bonds, group cohesion and task cohesion, in ensuring mission success. What commentators do note, however, is that the formation and performance of unit cohesion is not necessarily unproblematic. Certainly in the *Women in the Armed Forces* report, unit cohesion is prioritised as the *sine qua non* to effective infantry operations, beyond dispute as a factor that can ultimately determine operational success or failure. Yet unit cohesion is not as unproblematic an issue as the report suggested. As Joshua Goldstein points out, there can be operational effects as a result of too much social cohesion.[53] Research on the Israeli Defence Force's engagements during the Al-Aqsa Intifada suggested that in 'instant units' composed of changing personnel pulled together quickly for specific engagements, operational effectiveness relied on factors other than traditional organic modes of cohesion that are commonly understood to glue together more established units, factors including trust, expertise and shared knowledge.[54] Research on cohesion issues conducted by Tony King amongst British Royal Marines also problematises the idea of informal practices that constitute social cohesion as the primary basis for unit cohesion and operational effectiveness. He argues instead that formal practices around the formal processes of training, particularly communication drills, form the basis of operationally effective cohesion.[55] So, although unit cohesion is clearly a factor in operational effectiveness, we need to be aware of the discursive (and thus political) consequences of these arguments.

A second point about the exclusion of women from direct combat positions is the essentialist understanding about women upon which the policy rests. At the heart of the policy is a representation of women as threatening to unit cohesion not because of anything they may do (or be unable to do) in practical or material terms – indeed, the report is clear that, although the proportion of women able to reach required physical standards for infantry posts would be tiny, nevertheless some women would be able to achieve those standards.[56] Women who participated in direct combat units would be assumed to be as physically capable as their male team mates. It is their very presence, as women, that is understood as disruptive. Ultimately their difference is held to be the key factor incompatible with performance in the bonded male team.

It is interesting to consider this in view of studies drawing on the experiences within the US military that emphasise male activities such as sexual harassment as a significant factor affecting cohesion when measured through statistical correlation. A hostile work environment has been associated with lower combat readiness and high levels of sexual harassment correlate with low levels of preparedness for operational missions.[57] Studies conducted for the US Department of Defense by the RAND Corporation, a research institute not known for its radical political views, concluded that gender differences did not erode cohesion; cohesion was high when people believed that commanders emphasised unity and the importance of the roles of all members in achieving mission success.[58] Men and women can work together effectively in military units, the report argued, if women feel that they will be treated equally and if men perceive that women do not receive special treatment. Leadership is a key issue, rather than difference. The importance of leadership in the establishment of equitable (and thus militarily efficient) regimes of military organisation is emphasised as a defining factor by the MoD in its current actions against sexual harassment (which we discuss below).

It is also interesting to compare female difference with other differences that in the past have been represented as threatening to unit cohesion. Differences in skin tone, in cultural background and in sexuality have all at various times been marked out as potentially incompatible with the development of unit cohesion. Most recently in Britain, for example, arguments against the inclusion of 'out' gay men in the armed forces rested in part on the idea that the very fact of their sexuality marked out a difference that could not be accommodated and which would undermine the performance of the combat unit. Following the lifting of the ban on the employment of gay personnel after a ruling by the European Court of Human Rights in 2000, sexuality (in policy at least) became a non-issue in the armed forces, and there have been no public statements or reports (that we can find) that have indicated an deleterious effect on unit cohesion or operational capability as a consequence of the co-participation of straight and gay men (or lesbian women) working together.[59] It would seem that female difference is significant in ways that other differences are not.

Sexual harassment

There is now considerable evidence and public debate around bullying and harassment as a feature of Army culture. The framing of equal opportunities and diversity policies around the prohibition of harassment and the identification of harassment as incompatible with military effectiveness is perhaps indicative of this. Internal research such as the Army's Continuous Attitude Survey for 2003 reported 10 per cent of the sample claiming to have experienced bullying and 17 per cent claiming harassment of some kind.[60] A MORI poll commissioned by the MoD in 2005 reported 10 per cent of respondents claiming to have been bullied and 9 per cent reporting harassment.[61] Significantly for the Army, harassment and bullying have become issues of public debate in the past decade, with popular representations of an intolerant and abusive culture bolstered by the ready availability of stories of abuse, whether revealed in industrial tribunal or through media exposé. Arguments that Army life necessarily involves a degree of personal abuse because military training requires it, have given way to a public discourse of concern about the prevalence and severity of both bullying and harassment. The bereaved families of four young soldiers, who died in separate incidents over a five-year period at Deepcut Barracks in Surrey, have raised publicly questions as to whether these deaths were purely accidental or they were indicative of a wider, and tolerated, culture of bullying at the barracks. A House of Commons Defence Committee report on the Army's duty of care towards its young recruits stated its concerns that reported levels of bullying and harassment belied a greater prevalence of these practices.[62] Much of that harassment is sexual in nature. As we have already noted, the ALI's investigation into Army training was highly critical of a culture in which discriminatory practices were accepted as part of Army life, when there was little evidence that such practices actually brought appreciable operational benefits. The ALI was dismissive of the Army's efforts to address equal opportunities issues around combating bullying and harassment; it noted how a lot of the behaviour that it interpreted as harassment was actually condoned as part of an Army tradition, and emphasised that women and members of minority ethnic groups were particularly vulnerable. It noted how, although much harassment was perpetrated by recruits on other recruits, it was sometimes the case that staff were also implicated. Quite simply, the Army was not doing enough to control bullying and harassment.

Both the House of Commons Defence Committee's and the ALI's reports, then, pointed to the prevalence of sexual harassment and bullying despite the introduction of equality and diversity policies which had been intended to address the issue. In June 2005, using its statutory powers, the EOC formally put the armed forces under investigation, an action immediately suspended on agreement with the MoD that action would be taken to both prevent and deal effectively with sexual harassment in the armed forces. A key action taken by the EOC and MoD was to commission research into the prevalence of sexual harassment. This was published in May 2006, and provides a comprehensive overview of the experiences of personnel across the services.[63] An action plan was put in place, which is being implemented at the time of writing, to try and address harassment issues.[64] In agreeing with EOC requests for a full investigation and definitive action to combat the problem, the MoD was making, in effect, a public declaration about both the prevalence of harassment and its problematic nature.

The research findings were based in a survey of all servicewomen, with a response rate of 52 per cent. Quantitative data were combined with qualitative data from focus groups with both men and women personnel. The study found that sexualised behaviours, including jokes and anecdotes, language and materials, were widespread, and almost all survey respondents had been in situations where sexualised behaviours had taken place, in the 12 months prior to being surveyed. Although there was a high level of tolerance for these behaviours, over one-half of the survey respondents said that they sometimes found them offensive, with highly explicit sexual language, details of sexual exploits and the display of pornography identified as the behaviours most frequently found offensive. Over two-thirds of the respondents to the survey reported that they had encountered sexual behaviours directed at them personally, behaviours that included unwelcome comments, the distribution of sexually explicit material, unwanted touching and sexual assaults. Young women were more likely to experience such behaviours. The research also suggested that there was a lack of awareness amongst men that women could be offended or upset by their language or behaviours. Around 15 per cent of survey respondents reported having had an experience that they found particularly upsetting in the previous 12 months, and sexual assault was cited by about 12 per cent of respondents. Overall, 42 per cent of the survey respondents felt that there was a problem with sexual harassment in their particular branch of the armed forces, whereas most of the men involved in focus group discussions did not feel that there was a problem.

There are three points that we wish to highlight around this survey. First, through qualitative research undertaken in order to contextualise the findings on sexual harassment, the research produced evidence around the questions of female difference which complements our discussions above about the construction of female difference in policy language. In focus group discussions with male service personnel, exaggerations of female difference around physical attributes were used to consolidate arguments hostile to women's military participation. Specific traits and characteristics associated with the armed forces (such as bravery, physical strength, leadership abilities and a willingness to follow orders) were emphasised as masculine. In a service environment constructed as essentially macho and physically demanding, women were often viewed as a liability and not physically or emotionally strong enough to do the job to the required standards. Female difference was presented as contrary to the ideal, what the report terms the 'negative exaggeration of difference'.[65] These findings are supported by the ALI's investigation into safer training, which talked of a 'confused perception of women' underpinning a culture of harassment in the Army.[66]

The British Army is not alone here. There are echoes of these ideas in the experiences of the US Army. There is evidence of an often brutal misogynistic culture pervasive across the US military establishment.[67] Research by Laura Miller has concluded that men, despite their training and a general prohibition, can resort to sexual harassment, often very covertly, as a means of expressing their disapproval of women's military participation. When that harassment is covert it is harder for military authorities to tackle. Miller argues for the existence of a perception in this socially dominant group of military men that they themselves are oppressed, deploying resistance strategies, 'weapons of the weak' more commonly associated with subordinate groups as a means of expressing their resistance within a context where overt resistance is discouraged.[68] That discouragement, argue Firestone and Harris, with its focus on addressing individual behaviour, does not address the masculine environmental context that provokes those behaviours, so ultimately there are limits to what policy prescriptions can achieve in tackling sexual harassment.[69]

The second point concerns the MoD and EOC survey's findings on the continual sexual objectification of women, as a means of emphasising their unsuitability for military participation and as a means of emphasising the men's sense of superiority. Reported strategies included attributing female success to the granting of sexual favours. The research also comments that the sexual objectification of women was construed by many men as acceptable. For Melissa Herbert, writing about the intersections of gender and sexuality in the lives of US military women, the broader ideologies around gender, such as this kind of sexual objectification, are much more effective in limiting the participation of women in the military than either specific institutional or interpersonal constraints. This puts many military women in an almost impossible situation: 'Women in the military must do gender in such a way as to carefully negotiate terrain that often appears designed to make the venture as difficult as possible.'[70]

Our third point is to raise questions about wider appreciation of the cultural context in which sexual harassment takes place, within the Army and the MoD policy debates. The research commissioned by the MoD and reported here is hard hitting and provides a wealth of evidence to suggest that sexualised behaviours are interpreted by many women personnel as upsetting and harassing. These findings were duly reported in the MoD's own assessments of the nature of the problem, represented as an evidence base about the prevalence of harassment, upon which strategies set out in an action plan could build to address the issue. What is interesting is that, whereas the research clearly locates the practices and prevalence of sexual harassment to the Army's own cultures around gender, the MoD's action plan that draws on this research makes no mention of this cultural context. The MoD is not dismissive of the idea of gender cultures being significant in promoting fair working conditions; one of the strategies of action outlined by the MoD, in consultation with the EOC, was to look more explicitly at male behaviours as a factor in sexual harassment, which suggests that cultures around male behaviours are recognised as problems. Although not dismissive, there remains little public discussion of the significance of cultures of gender in shaping the wider context within which gender relations are played out. This is the focus of the next chapter.

4 Masculinities and the British Army

> To put it plainly and simply, my reason for joining up was that I wanted to become a real man.[1]

In Chapter 3 we looked at discourses on gender that circulate through policy. This chapter turns to the way that gender identities are made and remade within the contemporary British Army through its cultural practices. Focusing first on masculinities, we consider what these British Army masculinities are like, and how they are lived, embodied and performed through the formal and informal practices involved in Army training, work and culture. In doing this we draw on a body of work that has begun to bring recent theoretical work on gender and embodiment to bear on the examination of military masculinities.[2] We go on to consider what it means when women soldiers inhabit this masculine culture and its practices.

The statement by former paratrooper Ken Lukowiak at the head of this chapter indicates the way in which the idea of becoming a soldier is intimately tied up with the idea of becoming a man. And not just a man, but a privileged kind of 'real man'. As David Morgan puts it, 'the warrior still seems to be a key symbol of masculinity.'[3] One idea found in writing about military masculinities is that here, in the figure of the warrior-hero, we find the most extreme expression of hegemonic masculinity, characterised by 'the interrelationship of stoicism, phallocentricity and the domination of weaker individuals, competitiveness and heroic achievement'.[4] Recent work on masculinity, however, has highlighted that masculinity is not singular or monolithic, but plural and diverse.[5] This is indeed the case with military masculinities, as Higate and others point out.[6] The widely circulated masculinity of the warrior-hero is not the only military masculinity; the figure of the warrior-hero is accompanied by a range of other figures of the soldier that may be dominant or less dominant in different historical and cultural contexts: the soldier as peace-keeper, as professional, as stereotypical 'squaddie' and so on. Connell has argued, for example, that it is the relationship between different forms of masculinities that forms the basis of much military organisation.[7]

Theorists of masculinity have also argued for the need for masculinities to be conceptualised in ways that are historically specific.[8] Just as multiple masculinities exist within the Army at any one moment in time, so they change with time. The idea that masculinities shift and change is perhaps in tension with the notion of 'tradition' that is so important to the identity of the British Army, an institution which gives importance to the maintenance of 'traditional', longstanding practices and institutions. In its discussion of the conditions of work in the infantry, for example, the Army's recruitment website states that:

> Life in the Infantry involves much outdoor work in all weather conditions, long hours on exercises and sometimes on operations. Remember that you will not be alone. You will be part of a long tradition of the British Infantry always serving as part of a team in a regiment that is rightly proud of its soldiers and takes good care of them.[9]

Here the idea of tradition is invoked as a support for the soldier undergoing the rigours of the infantry role. He is invited to reflect that in enduring those hardships he is part of a long tradition. This also implies that those qualities of teamwork, toughness and stoicism that are developed through and for such rigorous conditions have a long history: in other words, it implies a reference to and continuation of older, 'traditional', practices and models of masculinity. At the same time, there is a recognised need for change in how soldiers and their masculinities are defined, alongside shifts, for example, in operational requirements, recruitment needs or legal challenges by bodies such as the Equal Opportunities Commission (EOC). We can see, for example, how the representations of military masculinities offered in Army recruitment advertisements shift according to the context.[10]

Another key strand in contemporary writing on masculinity is the idea that masculinities are not only produced in their difference from other versions of masculinity, but are also defined through their relationship to femininity.[11] Military masculinities are produced through other relations too: with the enemy, with other forces (particularly 'The Americans'). Bibbings shows how during the First World War the soldier was defined in relation to the figure of the conscientious objector: 'if the military man was brave, loyal, patriotic, self-sacrificing and true the [conscientious objector] had to be cowardly, disloyal, unpatriotic, selfish and traitorous'.[12] Connell also argues that hegemonic masculinity is 'aggressively heterosexual. It defines itself in part by a vehement rejection of homosexuality'.[13]

The final set of ideas about gender that we refer to turn on the notion that gender is not something we are but something we do, something we perform. Gender is performed and constructed in an ongoing fashion through, as Butler puts it, 'a stylized repetition of acts'.[14]

Features of British Army masculinities

What do contemporary British Army masculinities look like? One starting point for considering this is to look at the representations of the soldier that are produced and circulated by the Army for recruitment purposes. These are representations produced for a particular purpose, for recruitment, but also to project an image of the British soldier on a national and international stage. They offer an institutionally sanctioned representation of the British soldier, for public circulation.

If we look at the recruitment pages of the Army's website, we see a set of images and descriptions of different roles and careers within the Army which highlight the multiplicity of roles within the organisation. These are categorised under the seven headings of Combat, Engineering, IT/Comms, Officer, Logistics, Healthcare, HR, Admin & Finance, and Specialist.[15] A further series of job types are found nesting beneath these broad categories. Within the 'Combat' category, for example, are five further categories: Infantry, Army Air Corps, Household Cavalry, Royal Armoured Corps and Royal Artillery (which itself includes a further eleven jobs). Although these categories are offered here simply as employment areas, the representations of these roles also imply different kinds of gendered identities or, more specifically, masculinities. This can be seen first in the photographs that accompany each job type. 'Combat', for example, is illustrated with a picture of a male soldier in combat dress, looking through the sight of a gun. He is out of doors, with trees in the background. In contrast with this outdoor 'man of action', the category of 'HR, Admin & Finance' offers a more white collar image of a male soldier situated indoors, in combat jacket but bare headed, sitting at a desk and engaged in conversation with another person, with a computer in the background. This image suggests interpersonal communication and organisational skills. The masculinities associated with these different Army roles can be further read from the job descriptions attached to each job type. The Combat position of Tank Crewman/Mounted Dutyman in the Household Cavalry, for example, is characterised as occupied by 'intelligent, fit and decisive soldiers who have a thirst for challenge and a passion for winning'. The Infantry Soldier, similarly, has to be 'tough, fit, reliable, adaptable and determined' with 'loyalty and a sense of humour' and 'flexibility of mind'. These might both be compared to the masculinities contained in roles such as that of Military Clerk, who 'must have a genuine interest in providing support to others. A quick and orderly mind and the ability to pay attention to detail' and, above all, to be 'trustworthy, hardworking and team-orientated'. That these different gendered identities exist within a hierarchy of value with Combat-related masculinities at the apex, is explicit: the Combat role of Household Cavalry Tank Crewman/Mounted Dutyman, for example, is described as 'one of the elite of the Army'.[16]

While being mindful of the range of masculinities represented here, we can point to some features of British military masculinities that run through and across them, even if some features are more or less dominant in different places. As the recruitment text indicates, even a specialist musician is 'a soldier first and foremost', and all soldiers attend 12 weeks of basic training, the 'Common Military Syllabus (Recruits) [CMS(R)]', which is designed to inculcate a set of common skills and values.[17] The Common Military Syllabus and associated manuals make it quite clear what the characteristics of the trained British soldier are. The following is taken from the 'Code of Practice for Instructors':

> The British Army has a very special training ethos. It is a mixture of sharp

> discipline, tough training, maintenance of high standards, a sense of fair play, treating the trainee as an individual and encouraging people to achieve things far beyond what they thought themselves first capable of. Skill, strength and forbearance are admired, whilst brutality, callousness and meanness are despised. Our training is characterised by a strong sense of humour and by compassion for the less able. The training is successful if it results in a high level of skill, self-discipline, initiative and obedience to orders in the moment of crisis.[18]

Hence, the Army Training Regiment Winchester [ATR(W)], for example, can confidently claim that 'the 12 week progressive CMS(R) programme at ATR(W) produces individuals of the type described above'.[19] There are fifteen specific areas of training, covering the training of body and 'character', and the acquisition of military knowledge: Skill at Arms, Fieldcraft, Physical Training, First Aid, Nuclear Biological and Chemical (NBC) Training, Map Reading, Drill, Health and Hygiene, Adventurous Training, Military Education, Character Training, Financial Matters, Security, Military Law and Welfare. Implicit in all of this are attributes such as the ability to deploy controlled violence and aggression, stoicism, (endurance and 'soldiering on'), teamwork ('Be part of a highly motivated team pulling together to get the job done')[20] and professionalism.

This is the official and public discourse on what the British soldier is, accessible via public documents such as websites. These characteristics, it has been argued, are tied up with the production of, specifically, military *masculinities*,[21] and we will consider this further as we go on to examine the practices through which soldiers' gendered identities are made and maintained.

Practices

So if British Army masculinities can be seen to have particular features, and those masculinities are understood as something that is constructed and performed, then how does that process take place? Here we ask: How are these British military masculinities produced? Through what kinds of practices do soldiers come to live, to embody these military masculinities? We will look at a range of practices, ranging from the formal institutional practices, such as training processes, which are explicitly designed to inculcate particular skills and modes of embodiment, to the informal practices that work alongside them to make soldiers what they are. Bearing in mind our points about the multiple character of these masculinities, it is not our intention to provide an exhaustive or systematic mapping of all the varieties of cultural practices associated with the British Army. We will, rather, draw out some key ideas focusing specifically on the practices associated with one particular set of roles. We have chosen to focus on combat soldiers, because of the symbolic importance of the figure of the combat soldier as the 'ultimate' soldier, the 'real soldier'. In the range of military masculinities these are considered to be its most extreme manifestations – the most masculine, if you like – and include the roles from which women are still excluded. This may be at the risk of underplaying the significance of the other kinds of military masculinities to be found within the British Army.

This is also a matter of the sources that are available to us. Recent or substantial ethnographic research on the contemporary British Army is thin on the ground.[22] We draw here on two main kinds of sources. Our first source is John Hockey's ethnographic study of the infantry. This relies mainly on data collected during a period of three months of participant observation with Army units during 1979–80, and includes more recent re-readings of this material by Hockey with reference to issues of masculinity and embodiment.[23]

Our other main source is the personal testimony contained in soldiers' memoirs; published autobiographical accounts of soldiering.[24] There is a range of opinion on how these soldier narratives can and should be read, reflecting debates within literary studies over the use and critique of autobiography and memoir.[25] One view of these soldiers' narratives is that they constitute one meta-narrative – in Hynes' view, 'the soldiers' tale' – that is celebratory of the authenticity of the combat soldier's experience, and the consequences of such activities for the individual.[26] Others are more cautious, alert to the partiality of memory, the motivation and intentionality in their writing, and the politics of their production and consumption.[27] Alert to their readership and market, these narratives ground themselves on assertions about their 'truth' (however fantastical this might appear to the reader) and do so through their presentation of the self, the narrator, as ordinary (however extraordinary that person might be) and thus believable. These assertions about their 'truth' are important for marketing purposes; the stamp of authenticity guarantees sales to a readership intrigued by questions about what military violence is actually like.

In using these narratives as a textual source, we have to be alert to the claims about 'truth' that are inherent in a genre that is aware of its role in speaking to a wider readership, while remembering that, like all memoirs, they are inherently partial and selective. This tension in the act of reading does not necessarily close off these narratives as a source of information and reflection about military issues. These narratives are not just about 'telling it like it is' (a common assertion in the genre) but are also strategic engagements with dominant discourses shaping widely shared beliefs about the national significance of specific military actions. Our second point is about who writes, and does not write, narratives about their soldiering experience. Harari argues that the writing of the soldier narrative is an act of self-preservation, a way of getting to grips with and understanding the aberrance of war. They are 'the means by which the dreadful events of war were recast into an acceptable story of a "normal" life'.[28] Furthermore, those who actually get down to it and write about their experiences are distinct in that they are those for whom war does not entirely contradict their pre-war expectations.

We should approach soldier narratives, then, alert to their purpose and function. Being aware of this emphasises the point that they should be read not as innocent tales of reality, but as strategic interventions. We should be alert, though, to how the conventions of the genre shape, enable and restrict the articulation of those ideas; there are epistemological and methodological limits to the use of narratives as a data source for the interrogation of ideas of soldiering, as there are with any empirical resource. Narratives are a cultural product, read for the ideas and meanings that they convey, and for the ways in which they engage or counter wider discourses about the meaning of the soldier. They are valuable for the exploration of the construction of meaning, in that they are self-conscious about their readership and reception. Their limitation, of course, is that (unlike interviews) we cannot ask questions back to their authors, or prompt for a greater degree of explanation.

Finally, we have also drawn to a small extent on informal conversations with soldiers and former soldiers. These sources all speak specifically about male soldiers, and about military masculinities as they inscribe and are experienced by male bodies.

The body

We start with the significance of the body to the production of military masculinities. Military training directly and explicitly targets the body, through its various practices.[29] Becoming a soldier involves developing a particular mode of embodiment; soldiers' bodies are disciplined, moulded, treated, trained and experienced in particular ways, and have particular kinds of attributes and skills.

We will focus first on this process of 'becoming a soldier'. The transition from civilian to soldier in the British Army is achieved through the period of basic training. This is constructed as a rite of passage in which the trainee's status changes as he is literally moulded and shaped, mentally, emotionally and physically, to take up the subject position of soldier.[30] The metaphor of breaking down recruits to build them up is commonly used in soldiers' memoirs to describe this process, and is used by Army trainers themselves.[31] Hockey argues that this is not just a transition from civilian to infantryman, but from boy to man, and that instructional staff explicitly link 'role effectiveness' to 'masculine potency'.[32]

The issuing of uniform begins the process of shaping the body. The uniform, argues Morgan, 'absorbs individualities into a generalized and timeless masculinity while also connoting a control of emotion and a subordination to a larger rationality'.[33] Uniform restricts and shapes the body into particular postures and configurations. As Virginia Woolf, in her novel *Orlando*, suggests, 'It is clothes that wear us and not we them; we may make them take the mould of our arm or breast, but they mould our hearts, our brains, our tongues to their liking'.[34] Military uniform not only shapes the body's external form, but how the body is experienced too – how the soldier experiences his embodiment. Hockey notes how uncomfortable military clothing is. It is rougher on the skin than civilian clothing; boots and equipment produce blisters. This is all an introduction to the physical hardship that the recruit will experience in basic training.[35] The wearing of uniform does not, however, in itself make a soldier. One officer described those in basic training to us as 'civilians in uniform'. It is the body-focused practices and tests to which the trainee is subjected that begin to turn him into a soldier. This emphasises the status of 'soldier' as a new identity position that is both awarded and taken up through a process of bodily discipline and testing.

Basic training is a rite of passage involving the change from one cultural state to another.[36] Hockey describes the rite of passage undergone by the infantryman in basic training, in which his status changes from civilian to infantryman. Exercises and tests like 'drill, circuit training, road runs, assault courses, aikido and forced speed marches carrying heavy loads of equipment' are used to build both physical and mental endurance – a toughening of body and mind.[37] Exhaustion, lack of sleep, exposure to the weather, hazards, deprivations and discomforts – these sufferings have to be endured and accepted. This toughness and stoicism ('soldiering on'), argues Hockey, is explicitly linked to masculinity. Failure to perform, or physical weakness, for example, is repeatedly linked with the feminine: 'Some of you are like old women . . . Act like men and not a bunch of wet tarts . . . You bunch of girls are always at the back'.[38] Adam Ballinger, in a memoir about training and selection for Special Forces, refers repeatedly to the equation drawn between failure on the course and effeminacy: failures are called Girl Guides, queers, and fairies.[39]

Hockey observes that, although in basic training the masculinity that is privileged tends to approximate that of the warrior-hero model around which the representation of the soldier is organised, in actual operational situations the parameters of this model are amended in the interest of survival. He points to the use of the term 'hero' as a pejorative term for a soldier who takes unnecessary risks, putting his mates in danger. Here, he implies, the imperative of group solidarity and mutual cooperation over-rides the more individualist aspects of the 'warrior-hero' position. These characteristics of military masculinity and their relative dominance can be seen, to a certain degree, to be fluid and changeable.

Male bonding

'Group bonding', referred to as 'esprit de corps', is of prime importance to the identity of the British soldier, and 'teamwork' is one of the features most often mentioned in the job descriptions on the Army recruitment website. We have seen in Chapter 3 how male group bonding is privileged in policy discourse as a prime contributor to combat effectiveness. This is a longstanding practice: Bourke, for example, notes how attempts to stimulate 'male bonding' in servicemen during the First World War were made through disciplinary devices like 'the use of uniforms, ritualised humiliation and rites of powerlessness',[40] as well as through practices like the encouragement of public nudity, to which we will return.

There is a strong bodily dimension in the development of the bonded team. Hockey shows how this bonding is developed from early in basic training through activities such as helping exhausted mates carry their loads on a march, and moves into operational activities such as covering each other's movements on patrol and sharing sparse rations. Soldiers become responsible for each other's bodily health and safety, and share bodily demands. One former infantry soldier recalled to us a practice during basic training where the so-called 'sick, lame and lazy' had to be physically carried out to the PE hall by their peers.[41] This practice is a graphic lesson in the need to pull one's own weight as well as an injunction against giving in to physical or mental weakness. Hockey points out elsewhere that, in the rite of passage of basic training, 'The body is experienced no longer primarily as an individual entity, but rather as part of a collective one, termed "section" or "platoon" and garbed in anonymous military camouflage.'[42] This is inculcated also as an experience of 'physical togetherness' that is achieved, for example, through the effective performance of drill, which produces a kind of 'muscular bonding'.[43] This metaphor of a group of men as 'one body' is captured on the army recruitment website, on which the Household Cavalry Tank Crewman/Mounted Dutyman is described as 'the eyes and ears of the army'.

Bourke has argued that group or public nudity was used as a way of stimulating *esprit de corps* during the First World War. This began in the recruiting office, and continued on an almost daily basis. 'Men walked about "starkers" while their clothes were fumigated. They bathed together. It was a truly "gladsome sight", Charlie May brooded, to watch hundreds of men "stripped to the buff" digging in a trench: "Big muscles and supple joints swelling and swinging with the rhythm of the pick."'[44] Routine nakedness as a body practice persists in the contemporary British military. One former Royal Marine told us that being naked together with other men is a completely normal part of contemporary British military life. He took care to emphasise the completely routine and non-sexual nature of this nakedness. Group nakedness is another body practice that works to produce the bonded team. Just as uniform 'absorbs individuals into a generalised and timeless masculinity'[45] so can male group nakedness, as an insistent reminder that the group are 'one body'; that is, male bodies. In his memoir of life as a marine, Stephen Preece offers the following anecdote:

> I went to the bar to order some beer and stood next to a four star United States Marine Corps general, who was dressed in uniform and quietly drinking his beer. I rapidly put my heels together and acknowledged his rank with respect. He smiled. 'Relax, son,' he said in a broad American accent. 'I'm off duty'. He then stood up and unbuckled his trouser belt, dropped his trousers and underwear, leaned forward and showed all of us his arsehole. 'Look. See, it's the same as yours when I'm off duty. Let's drink.'[46]

Male bonding extends here to UK–US military bonding, forged over the commonalities of the naked body.

Another off-duty act of group bonding, this time involving semi-nakedness, can be seen in the production and global circulation of a 'home video' by British troops in the Royal Dragoon Guards stationed in Iraq. On 17 May 2005, the BBC news website reported that the video had crashed Ministry of Defence computers, which could not cope when so many people tried to download it. The video, entitled 'Is this the way to Armadillo' was widely circulated via the Internet and currently resides on the video posting website *YouTube*.[47] It is a pastiche based on a video made by the British comedian Peter Kay for the charity fundraiser 'Comic Relief'.[48] The British Army's spoof, 'Armadillo', features Staff Sgt Roger Parr, who marches through the Al Faw camp, summoning up a procession of 'fellow squaddies' along the way.[49] The mood is jaunty and upbeat. The video is, or appears to have been, achieved in one long shot, with Staff Sgt Parr in the centre of the frame, as he jauntily marches/dances his way through the camp. In a bizarre and funny choreography, groups of his mates move into shot, join him on his way, and then exit as the next group enter from another direction. The video offers a humorous portrait and expression of teamwork, its structure allowing it to introduce different members of the team in turn; each dressed (or, often, largely undressed) in a parody of their military role. Two soldiers, for example, are dressed only in tiny pants, but wearing boots and carrying guns and equipment. The final event has two portable toilet doors swinging open with perfect timing to reveal naked squaddies sitting on the toilet. Despite its low-budget 'home video' feel, the choreography and filming of the whole event is a testimony to a level of organisation, planning and timing in execution – military skills and teamwork, in fact. Framed by the makers as a way of lifting morale at the end of a six-month tour in Iraq, the video manages, in the context of war, both to parody and to celebrate the performance of military masculinities, particularly the teamwork that is so important to them. The team appearing in 'Armadillo' are all men.

Humour is used in a range of ways to sustain group bonds, especially in the form of banter ('slagging') or cruel practical jokes. As Preece puts it in his memoir, 'It's when people stop the slagging and start being nice to each other that you have to worry'.[50]

McNab describes this:

> There was a lot of blaggarding going on. If you didn't like the music somebody was playing, you'd slip in when they weren't there and replace their batteries with duds. Mark opened his Bergen to find that he'd lugged a twenty-pound rock with him all the way from Hereford. Wrongly suspecting me of putting it there, he replaced my tooth-paste with Uvistat sun-block. When I went to use it I bulked up.[51]

McNab never lets this representation over-ride another enduring feature of the discourse of elite military masculinities that he is constructing, however. In recounting the allocation of rations for an expedition, he tells us that: 'Stan didn't like Lancashire hotpot but loved steak and vegetables, so unbeknownst to him was swapped the contents. He would go over the border with fourteen days' worth of his least favourite meal.'[52]'It was just a stitch,' he continues, 'once we were out there we would swap around.'[53]

Lukowiak's memoir presents humour, particularly sick humour and pranks (a dismembered foot put in someone's sleeping bag, photographs of soldiers taken with dead bodies) as a coping strategy:

> If young men are sent 8,000 miles from their homes, to fight a war in a place

> that none of them had ever heard of, then such things should be expected. Their bravado was just a cover for their fear. Their actions were brought about by the conditioning they had received, at the expense of someone's taxes, to be able to fight, fight hard, and be sure that they would win. Win for you also.[54]

He offers it not just as a way of coping with the hardships and deprivation of combat, but as a way of coping with the performance of military masculinity, 'the conditioning they had received'.

We have seen in Chapter 3 how the bonded male team is privileged as an important contributor to 'combat effectiveness', and how women are constructed as potentially disruptive of this male bonding.

'Letting go'

Hockey observes that periods of deprivation or hazard are marked at their end with rituals of 'letting go that he terms "blowouts" '.[55] These involve a collective spree in which there is a release of tension and a celebration of the infantryman's role, organised around 'booze, "birds" and brawling'.

Preece's memoir similarly involves anecdotes about drunkenness. Of one colleague he says: 'The strange thing about Billy was that no matter how much beer he drank, he wibbled and wobbled but he never fell down. Also like the rest of us, no matter how much beer he drank, he would be ready to do his job the next day, whether it was a twenty-mile run or an arduous and dangerous patrol out in the field.'[56] He talks of a drinking session with another 'Marine mate', Craig:

> 'Here, drink this, I've bought you a drink,' he smiled and passed me a bucket full of bitter. I laughed and grabbed the bucket from him. It was heavy to hold and held around twelve pints. To ease the burden of holding the heavy buckets we removed our socks, tied them together and then tied them to the buckets. We then used the socks like slings and held them around our necks.[57]

Preece gets so drunk that night that he ends up smearing excrement around himself, his room, the corridor and the bathroom in the barracks.

Vince Bramley, a paratrooper, in his Falklands memoir, similarly describes a ritual associated with 'letting go':

> The 'Dance of the Flaming Arseholes' was the finale of most piss-ups. A volunteer, who is either very brave or very drunk, stand naked on a table with a toilet roll or newspaper rammed between the cheeks of his arse. To the chant of 'Alla, zoomby, alla zoomby', the paper is lit by the nearest guy with a lighter. As the paper catches and the flames get closer to his rear end, the lad dances quicker and quicker. Normally, the volunteer's pubic hair is non-existent after this little routine. It might leave him sore, but it raises a

roarin cheer around the hall or bar if the lad has braved it long enough to satisfy the crowd.[58]

There is a carnivalesque quality to these stories of 'letting go', in their celebration of the unregulated body (the body that 'wibbles and wobbles', even if it doesn't fall down), and in the featuring of bodily excess and of 'low' bodily features like excrement and arseholes: what Bakhtin calls 'the material lower bodily stratum'.[59] These bodies of 'letting go' are the antithesis of the tough, disciplined and controlled military body. Theorists of carnival have pointed to its fundamental ambivalence: although it celebrates the breakdown or inversion of social control (in this case, military discipline), it can also be seen as ultimately reinforcing that control by providing a 'safety valve' that is contained and limited.[60] Although 'letting go' in this way is the antithesis of military discipline, the celebration of the ability to do one's job the next day also works to reinforce that disciplinary system. It shows that, despite 'letting go' in the evening, discipline and proper military masculine behaviour can be restored when necessary. Such episodes of 'letting go' might then be seen as a temporary escape from but also an integral part of the formal practices that produce military masculinities and disciplined military bodies. Although they offer a respite from, or temporary resistance to, the disciplines and bodily regulation of army life, they are still utterly concerned with the production of masculinities, however. Practices of 'letting go' might be seen as reinforcing essentialised notions of masculinity as wild and uncontrolled that underpin the disciplined, controlled military body/subject. This is Hockey's argument; that 'blowouts' celebrate the idea that hard drinking 'is what "real men" *naturally* do'.[61] The aggressive pursuit of 'birds' and 'brawling' similarly naturalise aggressive heterosexuality and violence as natural and inevitable masculine behaviours. Morgan similarly argues that the informal cultures of the military revolve around the construction of heterosexuality. He points, for example, to 'the ubiquitous pin-ups', which 'establish direct links between the bodies of women and the bodily needs of men'.[62]

Speaking of the 'blowout', Hockey is careful to point out that 'none of this is to say that the ordinary infantryman does not go for a quiet drink, or visit the cinema, or pursue more sophisticated and less dramatic hobbies'. He argues, however, that 'narratives of release from duty' are articulated through these practices of 'booze, birds and brawling'.[63]

The interdependence between official, disciplined, military masculinities and their carnivalesque inverted unofficial others, can be seen on the website 'Shiny Capstar: Home of the 1st Battalion Coldstream Guards'.[64] The website offers a report on the 'Inter Company Pace Sticking Competition' of May 2006. It contains a report of the competition, a 'traditional' test of military skill, performed for a judging panel, and a series of formal photographs featuring the uniformed competitors, both posed in their Companies and on the parade ground. Scrolling to the bottom of the page, we find a photograph described as the 'ShinyCapstar Babe of 2006'; this features a grinning middle-aged man in implausible drag and 'feminine' pose, dressed in St George's flag bikini, wig and ladies' boots, juxtaposed with upper arm tattoo and copious stomach hair. This carnivalesque inversion of the disciplined military masculine body is highly ambiguous. As Butler argues, drag has the potentially transgressive ability to foreground gender as performance.[65] We could see this whole event, then, its official and unofficial representations, as foregrounding the performance of military masculinities, both through the spectacle of military skill and through the spectacle of drag. We can, at the same time, see it as a celebration of those masculinities and as a misogynist parody of their 'other', femininity. It is important, here, that this is *implausible* drag, which serves not so much to undermine the normative boundaries of masculine/feminine but to shore them up. Of course this is a man parodying a woman, it says, even if he is poking fun at his own masculinity too – and here his obviously male body, resplendent in its hairy maleness. This leads us to the importance of performance in the construction of military masculinities.

Performance

We have already suggested that soldiers' gendered identities are constructed through performance, through repeated bodily acts and stylisations. There are constant references in soldiers' memoirs to the ways in which military training is so thorough that, in moments of real fear and real danger, 'training takes over'. This confirms that performance as a soldier is developed, honed, and constructed; it does not come 'naturally'. The element of performance is highlighted by the degree of visibility and visual scrutiny involved in these activities, from inspections of body and kit to ritualised performances on the parade ground for an audience seated on tiered seating.

Lukowiak's memoir highlights this element of performance, speaking of an incident in the Falklands. He is in a gully with a handful of others, taking cover from artillery and mortar fire. They hear a man screaming, a young wounded Argentinian soldier. They're scared and unnerved by the screaming and Lukowiak loses his self-control, threatening to kill him. When he comes to his senses, he realises that the thing to do is to try to get some Argentinian prisoners being held further down the gully to bring the man in from the open. They refuse, so Lukowiak and his companion, Bill, go and rescue him themselves.

> Bill and I both grabbed an arm and pulled the still screaming boy back across the position he had lost the use of his legs defending and into the gully.
>
> We reached the gully, and took time to get our breath back and then pulled the boy back down the hill towards the other prisoners. We dropped him next to the one who has earlier refused to come with us. As we were leaving I shouted at the boy who we had just saved, I told him that he was a fucking cunt and then I kicked hard at one of his wounded legs. You should have heard him scream. We returned to the gully. I have often wondered why I kicked the boy. Which is strange because I always knew – others were watching. I may

> have helped save him but I wasn't soft, I was still hard. See, I just kicked him. I was still a man.[66]

In his reflections on this incident, given in the context of a narrative of redemption, Lukowiak emphasises the way in which he saw masculinity – being a man – as something he needed to perform in front of his mates. The theme is continued in another reflection. In Goose Green, the post arrives and a friend receives a photograph of his wife and newborn baby. The group are startled to find an almost identical photograph from the possessions of a dead Argentinian soldier, of mother and newborn. The group become, in Lukowiak's description, compassionate. 'But our mood of compassion was soon broken. Someone picked up and put on his Hard Man Paratrooper mask'.[67] The group make a series of sexual comments about the Argentinian widow: 'The next few minutes were filled with various soldiers trying to outdo each other with boasts of what they would like to do to the Argentine woman.' He can't recall what he said,

> but I am sure that I said something. Something that I thought to be suitably hard. Something that showed to the others that I was one of them. One of the boys.
>
> If we had been alone, I like to believe that not one of us would have passed comments of a sexual nature about the Argentine woman, but we were not alone, so we behaved in the way that we had been conditioned to behave. Conditions that was done mostly by ourselves to ourselves.[68]

So military masculinities are constituted through a series of levels of performance, including performance that is ordered and directed, such as training or drill, and performance that is self-policed according to implicit codes and shared understandings of gender, such as the examples given above, It also includes acts of self-representation that may be more self-reflexive. It is to these acts of self-representation that we now briefly turn.

Typing 'British Army' into the search engine of the video-sharing website *YouTube* brings up 623 items. These are home-made videos and slide shows, most of which are made by, for or about British soldiers. They range from patriotic tributes complete with national anthem and Union Jacks, such as 'The Soldier's Creed' to humorous celebrations of British soldiering like 'Armadillo', discussed earlier.[69] Although such activities are not usually considered in accounts of the production of military identities, evidence suggests that it is routine for British soldiers to engage in practices of self-representation. These range from the taking, circulation and display of personal photographs and home videos, to the more longstanding practices of diary keeping, letter and memoir writing. The soldiers' memoirs on which we have drawn can, as we have discussed, be seen in this way. The examination of soldiers' practices of identity construction through self-representation is an under-researched area, although it forms the focus of an ongoing research project.[70] Initial results from that research indicate that gender is a significant axis around which these narratives and representations of soldier identity are constructed.

Consequences

As David Morgan points out, then, traditionally 'combat and military experience separate men from women while binding men to men' and we have shown some of the ways in which this takes place. Morgan also goes on to remind us that 'it is also important to note the darker, less publicly celebrated associations of such institutions and events';[71] the linkage of rape and war, for example, or the sexual aggression that often accompanies the bonding of soldiers. The routine and humorous nakedness that accompanies activities of male bonding like the Armadillo video has an unhappy echo, for example, in the enforced nakedness of the Iraqi prisoners caught on camera in the 'abuse' incidents at the aid camp known as Camp Breadbasket in May 2003, which resulted in the conviction of three British soldiers. The evidence included photographs of naked Iraqi men simulating anal and oral sex for the camera; conflations of foreign and sexual otherness staged by their British captors for the camera. See also Paul Higate's nuanced analysis of cultures of military masculinity in relation to prostitution and peace-keeping in sub-Saharan Africa.[72] While our account has focused on one central kind of military masculinity, Higate's work also serves to remind us again that military masculinities are many, emphasising as it does the nuances and differences within military masculinities.[73]

Military femininities, female masculinities, military women

We now turn to the issue of the gender identities of women soldiers in the British Army. We have outlined in Chapter 2 how women's participation has taken shape up to and in the contemporary moment. So how can we understand women soldiers' engagement with military identities that, as we have seen, have a long history of being constructed, through formal and informal practices, as military masculinities and that take the male body as their norm? In comparison with military masculinities this is a relatively unexplored area, and in particular there is a lack of published academic ethnographic research that deals with the experiences of women soldiers in the British Army. The clumsiness of the terms proposed in the subtitle of this section – military femininities, female masculinities – reveals the awkwardness of the concept of the gender identity of the woman solder. How do we characterise the gender identity that she occupies? What positions are available to her?

In his analysis of the 'gender strategies' of US women naval officers entering the masculine workplace of the US Navy, Barrett identifies three discursive strategies adopted by the women. The first is a masculinising strategy, where women comply with masculine norms and adopt masculine discourse and practices. This adoption of masculine practices extends to the body: 'She strives to shape her body just as a man would, standing straight, squaring shoulders, deepening the voice.' He cites one woman: 'I wouldn't raise my voice. I cut my hair very short. I wore pants whenever I could. I even put on weight so I didn't have a girly shape . . . the men get respect, so I wanted to look like one'[74]. The second strategy he identifies is 'accommodating femininity': 'I never try to be one of the boys, use foul language, get drunk. I had a captain like that. She was a guy in every way. Everybody thought she was a dyke. She scared me. She was so rough. I'm a lady. I was raised to be a lady. I don't want to lose my femininity. I wear dresses. I wear make-up. I like being a woman. I like it when men open the door for me. I like it when they compliment the way I look.' The third strategy he describes as 'degendering strategy' where women attempt to create 'a neutral professional demeanour' in an attempt 'to disavow associations with either group of gender markers'.[75] He concludes that 'doing gender' is, for women officers, a delicate balancing act between being too masculine and too feminine. Some of Barrett's observations are echoed in Orna Sasson-Levy's analysis of Israeli women soldiers in masculine roles. Sasson-Levy's focus is on those women soldiers who fall into the first of Barrett's categories – the 'masculinising' strategy. She argues that these women shape their gender identities by mimicking combat soldiers' bodily and discursive practices, by distancing themselves from 'traditional femininity'.[76]

In discussing the representation of military women in Hollywood cinema, Yvonne Tasker refers to Halberstam's work on 'female masculinities'.[77] By this she refers to women who define themselves with reference to the characteristics of masculinity. Tasker cites Halberstam's comments on the experiences of 'masculine women' in the First World War, who gained

> the opportunity to live out the kinds of active lives that in peacetime they could only fantasize about. Although [Toupie] Lowther's ambulance unit was constantly hampered by conventional notions of female activity, they also did see active combat, and many of these women were applauded for the first time in their lives for behaving more like men than women.[78]

Tasker draws the reader's attention to the importance of applause here, making the point that, here, a 'militarized female masculinity . . . embodies both the transgression of gendered codes and a longing for belonging'. Orna Sasson-Levy makes a similar point about the 'longing for belonging' in her analysis of Israeli women soldiers in masculine roles:

> When women choose to integrate 'masculine' practices within their gender identities, they not only present a subversive feminine identity, but also identify and comply with the army's androcentric norms.[79]

A passage in Sarah Ford's memoir about participation in an intelligence unit operating in Northern Ireland illustrates something of the purpose of these distancing strategies. She is talking about her unease on hearing that she is to be posted to a unit with a reputation for being staffed by misogynists and 'chauvinistic Neanderthals', as she terms them. She meets a colleague, Liz, who initially misinterprets her worries as a lack of confidence in her professional soldiering abilities.

> 'Don't tell me – the map reading! I was the same as you. You'll be getting lots of practice in it.' I told her it was the sexism that bothered me more than the navigation, and she gave me one of her really dirty laughs. She was a rough little fucker. Short, stout, Cockney, muscled, she swore like a docker. 'They'll fucking put you through it! But don't worry about it, mate. They're just a bunch of chauvinist pigs. You'll be all right, but you'd better get your drinking up to scratch, 'cos you'll be in the bar a lot. If they start anything, just drop 'em. Show 'em who's boss.'[80]

Female masculinities, in this narrative, are presented as coping strategies to counter the male version.

Sasson-Levy argues that for women to adopt masculine identities is potentially 'subversive' in that it can disturb gender norms, reveal the contingent, performative nature of gender, and can even work to parody and undermine naturalised masculinity through its performances. At the same time, it ultimately identifies with the ideology, laws, and rules of the military. And she goes on to argue that although 'their identity constructions might be subversive locally, it does not alter the military's gender regime. The ambivalence and "gender chaos" they stir up . . . do not alter the pattern of gender power relations in the army.'[81] The concept of female masculinities has largely been developed in relation to deliberately gender transgressive practices such as female drag kings. It fits less comfortably with a scenario like the Army where women wish to take a place in a traditional and conservative masculine institution and where their presence, as we have seen in Chapter 3, is also constructed through an essentialist discourse of 'female disruptiveness'.

The options for women in their development of a soldier's identity are limited by both institutional constraints that construct her gender as 'limiting' or 'disruptive' and symbolic constraints (what models of the woman soldier are there?). Our earlier observations about the range of masculinities represented in the idea of the British soldier mean that there are a range of possible gendered positions for the female soldier, depending on the job group she occupies – some of which, as we have seen, are more masculine (in the hegemonic sense) than others. And we have shown in Chapter 2, the greatest number of women work in arms or services where women have a longer tradition of employment, and only a very small proportion have encroached into the combat-related areas. Although the actual number of women in combat-related posts is small, their great symbolic importance is revealed by the way in which they regularly crop up as figures in popular culture. We go on to look at this in Chapter 5.

Conclusion

We conclude with an observation about tradition and change. Although we have been careful to point out the historically and culturally contingent and shifting nature of masculinities, we have also been struck by the continuities and similarities between different accounts of practices for producing military masculinities. In particular we are struck by the similarities between John Hockey's account, based on fieldwork done between 1979 and 1980, and that of David Morgan, based on his national service in 1955–7. The lack of any substantial contemporary ethnographic research makes it difficult to assess how the tension between tradition and change is being worked out in the Army now, although, as we will see in Chapter 5, military gender issues are very much being worked over in the realm of popular discourse and popular culture.

5 Gender and the soldier in the British media and popular culture

So far we have examined how female difference is constructed within army culture at an elite policy level (Chapter 3) and how gendered military identities are made through the practices of soldiering (Chapter 4). In this chapter we move to a consideration of how gendered figures of the soldier circulate in British culture more widely, focusing on the media as a key site for the public circulation of images, stories and debates about soldiering. We will examine some significant ways in which the figures of male and female soldiers have been imagined within key areas of the British media, looking at the ways in which they circulate discourses on gender in particular historical moments and examining their connections with those discourses and representations discussed in Chapters 3 and 4. We will argue that the figure of the soldier has functioned in the media as a significant site for the working out of debates and anxieties about shifting gender identities and roles. The chapter concludes with some reflections on the relationship between discourses on gender circulating within the culture of the army and those circulating through the media.

Media discourse and 'figures' of the soldier

This discussion makes some assumptions about the way the media work. In line with the approach adopted so far, it draws on the idea that media operate discursively, an approach that is advocated by Macdonald.[1] Rather than viewing the media as, for example, 'reflecting' a separately existing reality, media discourse is considered to be constitutive, helping us to construct versions of reality. Consider, for example, Macdonald's example of the media constructions of the death of Princess Diana in 1997. The dominant discourse constructed by the British media was that of an 'outpouring of national grief',[2] the idea of a nation in mourning. Macdonald points out some of the ways in which this media discourse promoted one particular version of the story, a version that involved selectively ignoring some information, such as the number of people pictured in the media reports who were there to participate in a sense of history in the making rather than mourning, or who were spectating tourists rather than Britons. The point here is that this media discourse is selective, producing one version of reality over other possible versions. Macdonald's approach does not, however, see media discourse purely as a simulation or free-floating construction with no basis in material reality. As Macdonald points out, the crowds on the streets were real enough, 'but it is equally hard to believe that public reaction would have taken the form it did without the persistently elegiac and canonising tone of the intensive media coverage'.[3] In other words, there is an interaction between media discourse and public behaviour, an interaction that is 'neither one-way nor simple'.[4] This allows us to move beyond any simple notion of 'media effects', or the evaluation of whether media representations are, in some simple way, 'right' or 'wrong', a 'true' or 'false' representation of a separately existing reality. Taking this approach allows us to view media discourses on gender and soldiering as rooted in particular historical and cultural contexts. It can allow us to look at such media discourses as shifting, and as related to wider public discourses such as those policy discourses examined in Chapter 3.

A further idea that will be drawn on in this chapter is the notion that particular 'figures' are produced through discourse and circulate at specific historical times. Foucault, for example, identifies the emergence in the nineteenth century, in relation to the mounting preoccupation with sex, of four figures: 'the hysterical woman, the masturbating child, the Malthusian couple and the perverse adult'.[5] Such figures, suggests Kathryn Woodward, may be thought of as 'the recurring 'subject-positions', characteristic of the particular period and discursive formation'.[6] Woodward utilises this concept for an analysis of the production in the 1990s of new figures of motherhood such as that of the 'independent mother'. As Woodward's analysis suggests, the media is a key site for the contemporary circulation of such figures, and this chapter will utilise this concept in its tracing of gendered figures of the British soldier that circulate in the British media from the early 1990s. It allows us to see these figures as related to wider discourses that circulate within different fields within the media – across newspapers and TV drama, for example, and more widely within policy discourse. These 'figures' can be read for what they say about popular understandings of what a soldier is, and for how they circulate ideas about gender in particular historical moments.

The British soldier in the media and popular culture

Contemporary British popular culture is shot through with images of and stories about soldiers. We currently see daily news reports of soldiering in the print and broadcast media. Bookstore shelves are stocked with novels telling soldiers' stories, both fictional[7] and non-fictional.[8] They appear on television in drama (*Soldier Soldier*, *Red Cap*, *Ultimate Force*), fly-on-the-wall documentaries (*Soldiers to Be*, *Guns and Roses*) and as reality television series (*SAS: Are You Tough Enough? Destination D-Day: The Raw Recruits*). They appear in armed forces advertising campaigns and roadshows (*We Were There*, *A Force For Good*). The cinema has provided us with memorable and influential representations of soldiers both male and, more recently, female (*GI Jane* (1997), *Courage Under Fire* (1996)). We can buy soldier dolls and military-themed computer games for our children. We can even dress in soldier-inspired clothes as the fashion industry offers us khaki combat trousers, camouflage print and other military-style clothing.[9]

From this huge range of sites we have selected for our main focus two key media areas in which soldiers have figured since the beginning of the 1990s. Our primary examples will be drawn from British television drama and the print media. We have chosen these because they are widely circulating and popular, and because they allow us to examine how the figure of the soldier is imagined and circulates across a range of genres – via popular drama, for example, as well as through the construction of news. We will look at examples taken from a range of tabloid and broadsheet newspapers, and from three key television drama series that have a British Army setting and span the period from 1991 to 2006: *Soldier Soldier*, *Red Cap* and *Ultimate Force.*

Soldiers and their wives: the British Army as a gendered cultural space

In October 2001 the bikini-clad celebrity Geri Halliwell was pictured in *The Observer* frolicking with 'military minder Wing Commander Mark Smith on the beach at Salalah, Oman, before giving a concert for British services personnel in the Gulf' (*The Observer*, 7 October 2001). Setting off Halliwell's slender, nearly-naked female body against the bulky maleness of her protector, the camouflaged and booted Wing Commander, this photographic image speaks of the gendered opposition between 'man–soldier' and 'woman–civilian' that has historically structured the gendering of soldiering in the British Army. As this example shows, this gendering of the soldier/civilian is still upheld and circulated within contemporary media representations, a gendering that casts women as other and external to the soldier, most typically as wives, mothers, girlfriends or, as in the case of Halliwell, 'forces sweetheart'.

To explore this kind of media representation of soldiering, we are going to focus here on the representations of soldiers and their wives that are found in the popular 1990s TV drama *Soldier Soldier*. This ran to seven series and 82 episodes between 1991 and 1997, at the time following Options for Change, when the British Army was undergoing great change, as discussed in Chapter 2. One viewer speaks on the Internet Movie Database of his memories of *Soldier Soldier:*

> I was living as an attached civilian in Germany when this series kicked off. Immediately my family and I could relate to the situations the characters found themselves in . . . My family and I watched every episode as they I think they were on Tuesday nights in the main service channel SSVC. Then when we left the army we were pleased to see ITV (a British TV channel) was showing the series also.[10]

It is interesting that this viewer remembers watching *Soldier Soldier* in the context of his army family, because it is the family life of the soldier that forms its main focus.

The opening credits for each episode of *Soldier Soldier* feature a sequence in which, in silhouette, the figure of a soldier is met by a child. He bends down to pick up the child in his arms, lifts it aloft, and a female figure enters the frame to make up the composition of a family group. This iconic image – the soldier returning home to his family – signals the series' focus on the domestic and family life of the soldier, and on its offering of a view of soldiering from the perspective of the family. The real action of the series is not military action, but domestic. Series one, for example, begins with the return of the soldiers home to barracks, and to their families, and ends on the night before they are due to leave again for 'jungle training'. The series is not mainly or directly concerned with military action in itself. For example, although the first series opens with the death in action of a British soldier in Northern Ireland this is not lingered on – the scene in question is very brief. The episode is less concerned with showing the action of the event itself than to focus on its repercussions for the emotional life of the officer concerned. So, while military action forms an external backdrop to and a frame for the world of *Soldier Soldier*, the series' main concern is with the everyday domestic lives of its soldier protagonists and their families, wives, girlfriends and children.

Soldier Soldier offers a representation of the British Army as an institution that is fundamentally ordered around male–female work–home dichotomies. Crudely put, the world of *Soldier Soldier* is a world in which the men are soldiers and the women are wives, mothers and girlfriends (with one exception, to which we will come later). The division between the masculine realm of soldiering work and the feminised domestic and sexual realm in which women 'take care of the delicate stuff', as one officer puts it, is repeatedly underscored in images and storylines that see the soldiers' wives and girlfriends in domestic settings providing domestic, emotional and bedtime support for their soldier men folk.

This is highlighted in episode four, in which the storyline has Colonel Tony Wilton taking part in a boxing competition. The Colonel's pep talk prior to the match emphasises the need for the boxers/soldiers to forget distractions while fighting: 'Remember while you're out there try and forget everything else. Forget the mortgage. Forget the payments on the car . . . Try and forget the girls, at least until tomorrow'. These signifiers of domestic life and the feminine are distractions that must be put out of mind for the duration of the fight. Meanwhile, the wives and girlfriends, who are barred from the all-male and assertively masculine space of this event (signified by the activity of boxing), enjoy a highly feminised and sexualised event – a lingerie party – together at home. The scene culminates in the women deciding to go and spy on the boxing. Ironically, they do so in a parody of military discipline: in order to see through the high window they organise themselves into a motorcycle display team-style pyramid so that Wilton's wife, at the apex, can see the fight. This image of the male soldiers taking part in a communal masculine activity organised around a fight, in a space from which women are barred, with their wives looking on from the outside, one of them still dressed in basque, stockings, and suspenders from the lingerie party, characterises the gendered cultural space of the British Army, as portrayed by *Soldier Soldier*.

Soldier Soldier works towards maintaining the gendered duality that opposes work and home, soldier and wife, man and woman. This can be further examined by looking at how it sits in relation to wider shifts within British television drama. In the 1990s there were two main changes in British television drama. First, there is a shift towards consumer-led drama series and away from the social commitment of authored, 'serious' TV drama. Examples of such popular, consumer-led dramas include *Heartbeat* and *Peak Practice*. These are characterised as popular, 'cosy' and undemanding viewing that does not seek to challenge the status quo in the tradition of the 'serious' British TV drama. Second, there is a shift towards dramas that are innovative in form or content. For example the US import *ER* or British products *This Life* and *Cardiac Arrest*. The formal and stylistic innovations of *This Life*, for example, include fast cutting, elliptical edition, tighter framings on characters, all of which have potentially destabilising effects.[11] These innovative TV dramas are often also concerned with questioning conventional gender constructions. For example the representations of the figure of the doctor found in *ER* and *Cardiac Arrest* show a loss of faith in 'the doctor' as a secure figure of masculinity.[12] If we look at how *Soldier Soldier* is positioned in relation to these shifts, we can see it as part of the first one – the shift towards popular, consumer-led drama. Its author, Lucy Gannon, is associated with this field. Typically characterised as 'undemanding' viewing, this kind of drama is not positioned as a serious, 'social issue' or socially questioning drama. Neither is it characterised by the destabilising effect of innovative TV style in camerawork, editing, etc. Although it offers some critique of funding cuts (through a storyline on the regimental mergers that followed Options for Change), it does not fundamentally question the status quo in terms of the gendering of army culture or, indeed, the politics of the military and military participation.

In *Soldier Soldier* the feminine world of family and domestic life is shown as providing support for the male soldiers. It is also, however, shown as a source of conflict and tension for them. Often they are torn by conflicting allegiances between regimental 'family' and domestic family. This is played out, for example, in the episode three storyline in which the Army are providing an emergency service to clear rubbish from hospitals during a strike. CSM Chick Henwood, whose brother is a striker, is torn between his allegiance to his regiment and to his civilian family. His mother challenges him: 'It's just a question of what matters most, your family or the bloody Army'. Similarly, on the birth of Tony Wilton's baby his mate says: 'look at him: top soldier, top boxer, reduced to a quivering wreck.' This is said with affection and approval: the perspective of the series seems to be that family/the feminine is both a necessary counterpart ('support') for the soldier's masculine identity and, at the same time, potentially disruptive of it.

By casting a spotlight on the feminised domestic 'underside' of this masculine institution, *Soldier Soldier* reveals how utterly dependent the identity of the soldier is on this other, on the institution of the family, on the feminine. *Soldier Soldier* also potentially foregrounds the notion that maintaining the identity of a soldier, maintaining military masculinity as an identity, is a struggle. By foregrounding its narratives of their emotional lives, *Soldier Soldier* also humanises its soldiers, offering representations of the British soldier that are sympathetically drawn, inviting the viewer's understanding and empathy.

In general terms, then, *Soldier Soldier* works towards upholding the 'traditional' gendering of soldiering. It also opens up a space for the exploration of the emotional and domestic dimensions of soldiers' lives, and offers a popular representation of British soldiers that humanises and sympathises with them, implying connections between the 'ordinary' soldier and the viewer. This, as we have seen in Chapter 2, comes in the context of the emphasis in the 1990s on peace-keeping and humanitarian roles.

There is one figure in *Soldier Soldier* that has been strategically ignored so far in this discussion, which has centred on the traditional gendering of soldiers and their wives offered by the series. This is the figure of Nancy Thorpe, who is a member of the Military Police (the 'Red Caps'). The figure of Nancy is an early British televisual representation of the woman soldier, appearing in the first series in the early 1990s, at the beginning of the period of policy change that we have discussed in Chapter 3. The figure of the woman 'Red Cap' moves from the periphery of this TV drama to the centre of another drama, *Red Cap*, in the late 1990s, and we will be examining this in a moment. First, though, we turn to the wider emergence in the British media of the figure of the female soldier.

The figure of the female soldier in the British media

From the 1990s the landscape of the media is increasingly inhabited by female soldiers. These have Hollywood incarnations such as those played by Demi Moore in *GI Jane* (1997) and Meg Ryan in *Courage Under Fire* (1996). The figure of the female soldier also appears in various forms across the British media at this time. British media representations of the female soldier, which appear in the context of the policy debates about the place of women in the armed forces that was discussed in Chapter 3, tend to cluster around two figures, and these have their crudest and most caricatured form in the tabloid press. These are, first, the female soldier as both sexualised and disruptive, and, second, the female soldier as an incomplete man or 'tomboy'.

The 'sexually disruptive' female soldier

When the 1997 announcement about the increase in the number of jobs open to women in the British Army was made, this prompted the appearance in the tabloid press of cartoons featuring crudely sexualised representations of women soldiers. For example, an offering from the *Daily Express* features a large-breasted, bikini-wearing 'Private Goodbody' lining up on parade alongside camouflage-clad male soldiers. 'Private Goodbody, the idea is to shoot the enemy, not knock them dead,' barks the drill sergeant. Another later example depicts a young boy playing with a set of toy soldiers that are naked female figures.

One step removed from this kind of crude parody are stories and images such as those appearing in *The Sun*'s 'Saucy Services Special';[13] along with features about female soldiers 'Capt'n Crumpet' and 'Sexy Sherry', the centrepiece of this issue is the story of 'Sexy Roberta Winterton, the first serving soldier to pose for page three. Topless'. This story had wide circulation in the press and national television news. The main focus of this feature are the images of Lance Corporal Winterton, who appears in army uniform on the cover and, kit peeled open to expose her breasts, on page three. The training processes that make the soldier's body are reinterpreted here as a sexualising makeover for the female body: It was the (gruelling training) course that gave her such a super shape. She said 'My boobs got smaller but firmer and my legs seemed to get longer . . . I think I am a bit like Demi Moore in that film GI Jane.' When Winterton refers to the figure of Demi Moore/GI Jane here, it shows how these media figures come to be taken as cultural reference points for talking about the emergent figure of the female soldier – in this case, it references the way in which the film *GI Jane* offers representations of the training of the woman soldier's body as masculinising ('my boobs got smaller') but also as eroticising ('my legs got longer').

The story that frames these images emphasises that Winterton's act of appearing in *The Sun* was a breach of military discipline, resulting in her facing six military charges. The association of the sexualised woman with disruptions of military discipline or operations is a feature of a number of news stories about women soldiers. In the same issue of *The Sun* is a story about 'randy Wrens' on HMS Sheffield: '4 of this frigate's Wrens have got pregnant after sex with their shipmates . . . Some of the Wrens are just sex-mad'. Another representation of the 'sexually disruptive' female soldier is found in the widely reported story of Lance Bombardier Heidi Cochrane, who hit the headlines in the same week as the Winterton story when she went AWOL with married Sergeant Jason Archer.[14]

Although a number of stories feature 'sexually disruptive' women soldiers who have breached army discipline or had inappropriate sexual liaisons with officers and workmates, another story features a woman officer accused of sleeping with the enemy. In a story entitled 'the spy who shagged me',[15] a woman TA officer is reported to have had an affair with a Russian intelligence officer while escorting him on peace-keeping duties in Kosovo. This female officer is characterised as an 'innocent girl' deliberately targeted by the 'dashingly handsome' lieutenant colonel. Naive and vulnerable to penetration by manipulative enemy forces, it is her sexual vulnerability that is seen here as potentially disruptive to national security.

Whether in cartoon or photographic form, the tabloids' woman soldier is often represented with an insistently or excessively female body, emphasising the breasts in particular. The image of breasts bursting out of camouflage implies that the female body does not fit the uniform or the job of soldiering. This echoes the military perception of breasts as 'appendages' to a soldier's body, a body that is understood as normatively male. Such images suggest that the terms 'woman' and 'soldier' just don't go together. The act of revealing the breasts asserts the incongruity of the image of woman in combat gear. The breasts also serve as an emphatic reminder that beneath the unisex camouflage uniform is a *female* body. In the contemporary British Army, camouflage uniform such as that worn by 'sexy Roberta' is worn by both men and women, hence perhaps the need to strip the female soldier, here in the realm of media representation at least, for a visible reminder of her female body and the shoring up of gender boundaries. This reduction of women doing the job of soldiering to sexualised figures is a continual process, examples of which continue to recur. For example, in May 2006 *The Sun* reported an incident in which a 'girl soldier' dubbed 'Combat Barbie' by her unit and by the newspaper, was given a commendation after grappling in hand-to-hand combat with an armed prisoner and restraining him.[16]

What we have outlined here is, then, the repeated characterisation of the female soldier as, first, sexualised (and often excessively so) and, in relation to that, as disruptive: of military discipline, of the maintenance of proper officer-rank relationships or of national security. It should be pointed out that this is most often a figure associated with the tabloid press, certainly in its crudest forms. Here the conventions for the representation of the woman soldier are those that frame the representations of women more generally in this context. *The Sun*'s 'page three', for example, is structured by a set of generic conventions for the representation of the half-naked female body. Winterton, as a woman soldier, is posed and framed according to these conventions. The emphasis in the representation of the woman soldier is, then, on the fact that she is a woman.

We would suggest that humour, parody and undressing are used here to work towards undermining the figure of the woman soldier, potentially containing her by rendering her ridiculous – only good for a laugh. This tabloid regime of representation might be considered by some to be trivial, unworthy of serious analysis. However, these crude manifestations of the theme of female 'sexual disruptiveness' serve to highlight a discourse on women, which, in subtler forms, has also been traced in the policy discourses around women's participation that were examined in Chapter 3.

'I never think about being one of the girls here': the 'tomboy soldier'

The other figure around which print media representations of women soldiers cluster might be termed the 'tomboy soldier'. Consider, for example, an article appearing in the *Daily Telegraph* 'Army brains and brawn attack the killing fields of Devon'.[17] This is a piece about the Army's work in managing the foot-and-mouth epidemic, featuring an interview with Major Belinda Forsythe, 'the major in charge of clearing away the carcasses'. It is accompanied by a photograph of three young women soldiers dressed in combats, sleeves rolled up for action, pen poised over a map. Two of them have short haircuts, Forsythe a neat bun, and they all gaze frankly at the camera, lips together, almost smiling. This image could not be further from the sexualised figures described above. These soldiers are pictured in the act of doing their job, rather than displaying their bodies as spectacle. In fact the article starts by denouncing the tabloids' representation of Major Forsythe as 'top Army totty', and emphasises the calm professionalism of these soldiers. Major Forsythe 'compares herself to a wily old farmer rather than a Page Three pin-up. "I never think about being one of the girls here. We don't have chats about make-up or diets. We're more likely to chat about rendering capacity" '. Although these female soldiers are neither sexualised nor shown as participating in feminine culture, neither are they excessively masculinised. The short haircuts are boyish, for example, with floppy fringes, rather than resembling the shorter haircuts of male soldiers. Their physiques are slight and boyish not bulky or mannish.

The tone of the story is one that is approving of these young female soldiers and the job they are doing. It is significant, however, that this 'approving' representation of women soldiers is constructed in the context of a story about a civil emergency, rather than a combat situation. The events on the 'killing fields' are described through battlefield metaphors: 'this 32-year-old Army officer first led her troops into battle against foot and mouth in Devon a fortnight ago . . . , But "Is it a war situation?" "No," she replies. "It's an emergency . . . the whole community has been devastated. In that way it is like a war." ' This characterisation of women soldiers as calm, efficient professionals is able to endorse their participation in a situation 'like a war', but avoids the question of whether it would endorse their full participation, as combat troops, in the 'killing fields' of a real war.

When the first women embarked on the Green Beret Commando training course, this was represented in the press as something of a testing ground for whether women soldiers would be 'up to' the gruelling training course required for this elite infantry role. The media representations of this process illustrate well the construction of this 'tomboy' figure of the woman soldier.

In a tabloid article entitled 'Gutsy Claire Knew She'd Had Enough', Captain Claire Phillips is characterised as a sensible girl, plucky, courageous and determined. She is characterised as deserving of respect for her bravery and determination but, in the end she is just not quite good enough, and she knows that: she knows when she's 'had enough'.[18] This figure, then, is brave, determined and capable but knows her limits. We have designated her a 'tomboy' because this captures the sense that she can impersonate a man, within limits, but can never actually be one. The tomboy figure is associated with a limited acceptance of female soldiers. Tomboy soldiers are often spoken of approvingly or affectionately. Their pluck and determination is praised. Built into the figure of the tomboy, though, is limitation. The tomboy can only ever impersonate a man but can never be a mature man. Ultimately, of course, what the tomboy lacks is a male body. This might suggest that it is not masculinity *per se* that is valorised within Army discourse, it is male masculinity – masculinity plus a male body – as discussed in Chapter 4. These 'tomboy' representations acknowledge, even celebrate, the achievements of women soldiers and their ability to do the job, but place clear limitations on that ability and on the sphere in which she can operate.

In the 'tomboy' set of representations, as with the 'sexualised disruptive' it is their female body that stops women from being complete or proper soldiers. It is either excessively, maturely, sexual (as in the sexualised figure) or it is lacking, immature or incomplete (as in the tomboy). By refusing to take the figure of the female soldier seriously, by insistently foregrounding her female body, by circulating stories of her disruptiveness, and by constructing her in terms of limitations, the female soldier is often, then, represented in ways that contain her power to disturb the gendering male of the soldier. These representations work to fix her as 'properly' female.

'But not all soldiers are men': women soldiers and 'female knowledge'

We turn now to an attempt to construct an alternative figure of the female soldier, one that originates in Army recruitment discourse and circulates in the media as a TV recruitment advertisement. *Torchlight* was an advertisement made by Saatchi and Saatchi for the British Army as part of their PR and recruitment campaign of the 1990s. *Torchlight* was notable as an attempt to address potential female recruits and, more generally, to market the Army as an 'equal opportunities' employer.

Torchlight is shot via a 'point of view' hand-held camera, in which the viewer sees the scene as if seeing it through the eye of the soldier. The scene is that of an unspecified (Eastern European?) village. The wreckage speaks of violated domesticity: a domestic interior, fragmented, seen by flickering torchlight, family photos pinned to the wall. A voiceover informs us that 'the enemy' have killed a woman's husband and raped her. The woman is seen cowering in the corner of a bedroom, babe in arms. Subtitles tell us that 'the last thing she wants to see is more soldiers'. But, as she sees the soldier who is the bearer of the camera's (and thus the spectator's) look, her face softens. We hear a female voice: 'It's alright, it's alright'. Subtitles appear: 'But not all soldiers are men'.

Torchlight makes effective play with the visual conventions of point of view, and attempts to undermine the viewer's expectation that the soldier's point of view is inevitably that of a man. The advertisement mobilises a key argument in the debate about women and soldiering: the argument that 'feminine qualities' of empathy or negotiation, for example, can enhance the work of the soldier, and that the idea of what a soldier is and does needs to be expanded, particularly in the 'peace-keeping' roles that came to the fore in the post-Cold War period. The woman soldier here becomes the face of the British Army as 'peace-keepers'.

This alternative image of the female soldier is interesting and highly ambiguous. It has the potential to transform, or at least extend, the concept of soldiering, by including qualities and knowledge designated as feminine. At the same time, it supports the essentialised linkage of men with soldiering and women with peacemaking and can support the ghettoising of certain feminised areas of work in the Army as 'women's work'. It should also be pointed out that *Torchlight* displays the kind of representational economy seen, for example, in Hollywood films, in which the representation of a female hero is frequently accompanied by that of a female victim. Also, the woman soldier of *Torchlight* is never visually represented. We are only given her point of view and her voice. While this is, on one level, a powerful device, inviting the viewer to imagine inhabiting the subject position of the female soldier, seeing through her eyes, it also means that we do not actually *see* the figure of the female soldier. The only female figure we see is the familiar representational figure of the mother/victim. The representational repertoire of

Torchlight, then, is organised around 'woman as victim of male violence' (rape), 'woman as mother' and 'woman as empathic peacemaker'.

The three figures that have been identified here sometimes appear as crude caricatures, especially in the tabloids, but are not necessarily distinct or mutually exclusive. Rather they form a kind of repertoire for representation. For example, Major Belinda Forsythe is constructed both as 'top army totty' by the tabloids and as 'tomboy' by the *Daily Telegraph*. This is also an indication of the extent to which the meaning of the figure of the female soldier is contested at this time, and subject to a struggle over meaning. Another example follows up the story of 'Gutsy Claire'. The following year, a woman soldier, Captain Pip Tattersall, succeeded in completing the Green Beret training course. The media discourse around this was interesting, because here the story could not be that the woman (tomboy) soldier had failed or recognised her own limits; Captain Tattersall had completed the training. Having reported her success, the reporting of the story then falls back on the discourse of 'disruptiveness'. Under the subheading 'Disruptive Influence', the story goes on to quote Major General Julian Thompson, who was quoted as saying: 'I'm not in favour of women being on the front line . . . I am sure there are women who are strong enough, but we are talking about cohesion of the unit . . . Women would be a disruptive influence on the team'[19]

If we look at the representation of the figure of the woman soldier in TV drama in the early twenty-first century, we see the intersection of these three figures of the woman soldier. *Red Cap* is a BBC television drama series that ran to two series and fifteen episodes between 2001 and 2004. It is significant for its representation of a military woman as its central character. As a professional woman, the character Jo McDonagh has many conventional hero qualities: she is highly professional and principled, and she also has a 'maverick' streak that sometimes sees her disobeying orders when necessary for solving her case.

The star-image[20] of the actress Tamsin Outhwaite brings glamour and sexuality to the figure of Jo McDonagh. This series was the major vehicle for her career after leaving the soap opera *East Enders*, during which time Outhwaite had won a British Soap Award for 'sexiest actress'. Outhwaite's 'sexiness' was part of the marketing for *Red Cap*, which juxtaposed images of the actress 'in training' for the part (training that took place with the support of the British Army), with more glamorous and sexualised images. She appeared on the cover of the *Radio Times*, for example, in a backless dress. The figure of Outhwaite articulates seriousness and professionalism (as an actor) with glamour and sexual attractiveness. She manages to be both professional and sexy, both serious and glamorous. It is through the star-image of Outhwaite and via these ancillary texts, that the figure of McDonagh is sexualised, while the series itself offers representations of the woman soldier that play down her sexiness through her businesslike clothing and demeanour. McDonagh's female sexuality is not generally seen as disruptive within this text. We do, however, find this discourse of 'female disruptiveness' circulating elsewhere in the texts through other female characters. Several of the series narratives revolve around figures of disruptive women. The discourse of 'sexual disruptiveness' thus hovers around the figure of McDonagh.

The figure of McDonagh is closer to the 'tomboy' figure, which is professional and capable but restricted or limited in some way. The main way in which McDonagh is limited as soldier – represented as not fully a soldier – is through her positioning as a 'Red Cap'. As such McDonagh is positioned as, ambiguously, both insider and outsider to army culture. This movement between 'insider' and 'outsider' status is marked narratively in her role as a member of the Military Police inhabiting but also charged with investigating and regulating military culture, and it is marked visually in her frequent changes between military uniform and civilian clothing.

Finally, McDonagh is frequently shown to use female knowledge in her detection work. For example, in one episode she smells and recognises a perfume that is missed by her male colleagues and provides a vital clue. Her femaleness here gives her valuable cultural knowledge that extends the possibilities of what a Red Cap can do. The figure of McDonagh/Outhwaite, then, articulates all three of these figures and their associated discourses on the feminine.

These figures of the female soldier are not simplistic or prescriptive. They do sometimes appear crudely as such in tabloids, cartoons, etc., but more often the media figure of the female soldier is a carrier of intersecting discourses. All of these discourses around the sexualised disruptive, the tomboy, the nurturing woman, rely on some pervasive and longstanding discourses on the feminine: the female body as inherently sexual; the feminine as disruptive; the female as 'other' to male norms; the female body as limited, lacking or incomplete; and woman as nurturing, empathic peacemaker.

Ultimate Force: 'smell the testosterone'

Since 2002 another British TV series has been telling stories focused on British military personnel. The popular series *Ultimate Force* had, by 2006, run to four seasons, although the fourth season was taken off the air after two episodes. Although *Soldier Soldier* had, in the early 1990s, set out to offer a representation of 'ordinary' soldiers from the perspective of their everyday lives, *Ultimate Force* is very much concerned with active service, with an emphasis on the *active*. As its title suggests, it is set within the elite British Special Forces, featuring the fictional Special Air Service 'Red Troop'. A first indication of its difference from *Soldier Soldier* can be seen from the generic categorisations applied to these series by the Internet Movie Database. *Soldier Soldier* is described as 'drama', *Ultimate Force* as 'action/war'.[21] Going alongside this generic classification with the masculine coded 'action/war' rather than the feminine coded 'drama', the language circulating around this series frequently highlights the way that it is seen by critics to be concerned with a 'macho' brand of masculinity. This is also how it markets itself. The first comment on the cover of the DVD of the third series, for example, quotes a *Mail on Sunday* newspaper review: 'More macho muscle power . . . smell the testosterone'.[22]

The opening credit sequence for the first series of *Ultimate Force* begins, like that of *Soldier Soldier*, with a group of figures in silhouette. This is, as with *Sol-*

dier Soldier, an iconic opening image. Where *Soldier Soldier's* grouping of figures was instantly recognisable as an image of the soldier returning home to his family, this image is instantly recognisable as that of a group of soldiers, uniformed, one with his weapon across his shoulders, composed in a line across the screen, backs to the viewer, walking away from the camera. They are set against the backdrop of a military compound, and viewed through a chain link and barbed wire fence, which suggests the separation of their military world from the 'outside' (civilian) world and from the world of the viewer, who watches from the outside, through the fence. This image signals the series' primary concern not with the soldier within his domestic family but with the soldier within his unit.

Ultimate Force characterises the soldiers and the masculinities of Red Troop by distinguishing them from and defining them in relation to a series of other groups. As suggested by the opening image discussed above, they are defined most fundamentally as separate from the civilian realm. This begins in episode one when the new team member Jamie has a visit from his sister Beth, who tells him that his mother is dying from a stroke and begs him to come home. Beth looks out of place in this military context. Everyone but her is in uniform; she looks windswept and uncomfortable. The arrival of Beth causes an interruption to the action of the training, and to the flow of the episode. This incident is treated by Red Troop's leader Henno Garvie as a particularly unwelcome interruption. In response to the commanding officer's offer of 'a couple of days leave', Garvie takes him to one side: 'Ill or dead? Dead is a couple of days. Ill is a phone call. We're on 30 minutes standby.' The civilian world, aligned here with the family and the feminine – the sister and the mother – intrudes into the televisual world and narrative of *Ultimate Force* and its presence is viewed as disruptive and unwelcome, standing for an emotional pull that is at odds with the soldier's responsibilities to his unit and his job. This is in contrast with the televisual world of *Soldier Soldier*, which often takes the tension between military and home life as the source of its drama. Whereas, in *Soldier Soldier*, the soldiers' families are always present and form an integral part of the drama, in *Ultimate Force* wives, girlfriends and families are narratively marginal and the source of the drama lies within the military action.

When Jamie arrives home (and his visit there is very brief, before he exits in a helicopter), the family home is occupied by women and by men whose masculinity is compromised. Apart from his sister and his dying mother, he is first greeted by his younger brother who has learning difficulties, and who speaks and behaves innocently like a very young child. When his father appears, he is bullying, fat and aggressive, treating Jamie to an unprovoked torrent of verbal abuse. It is strongly implied that his father had been violent towards him as a child ('You think you're big enough yet? Reckon you can take me yet?'). The father's masculinity is characterised by uncontrolled aggression, with hints of an unacceptable wielding of male power over a child, and housed in an unregulated, fat body. This is counterposed to Jamie's outwardly calm demeanour and fit, controlled body as he walks away from the abuse, and then runs to the waiting helicopter to a proud and admiring 'thumbs up' from his siblings. As the helicopter bears him away from this unhappy place, Jamie's elite soldier identity is figured quite explicitly as an escape from this world of his family, characterised by a femininity that is powerless and victimised – the mother is literally paralysed, his sister seems trapped – and masculinities that are weak, incomplete, uncontrolled and compromised. He has moved from this unsatisfactory civilian family, with its uncomfortable emotional responsibilities and unacceptable masculinities, into the bonded male 'family' of Red Troop, where the masculinity of Garvie, who becomes a kind of 'father figure' for him, forms a more acceptable model. Garvie says later in the episode: 'I can teach you.' He is speaking of teaching him to be a soldier, but the implication is that he is also teaching him how to be a man. The representation of this military unit as 'family' is underlined later in the episode when Red Troop sits down to a meal together, a visual construction of 'family'. As they settle around the table, the camera moves in on Jamie's face, and his expression as he looks around at them is one of contentment.

Red Troop are not only defined as 'military' in opposition to 'civilian', but also they are defined in relation to other masculinities within the army. Most typically, this takes the form of exchanges between them and the 'Ruperts' of the officer class. 'Never call a Rupert "Sir" ' is one of the first lessons Garvie teaches to the new team members Jamie and Alex. When, as protocol demands, Garvie is required to call officers (or Home Office officials) 'Sir' to their face, his tone of voice invariably drips with irony and contempt. Throughout the series Garvie frequently over-rules and undermines officers, as he authoritatively takes command of operational situations. In episode one, one of the first scenes in which Red Troop are shown together is when they are shown as united in their derision of their young commanding officer. There is clearly a class dimension to this distinction between Red Troop and their officers, hence their frequent use of the typically upper class name 'Rupert' to designate the officer. However, this is not simply a matter of class. First, this is indicated by the way in which the term 'Rupert' is frequently preceded by the qualifier 'inexperienced'. The distinction between Red Troop and their captain is a distinction that privileges operational experience. This is highlighted in an episode one scene between Garvie and the 'inexperienced Rupert' who has become their captain. Alone with Garvie, the captain says: 'I think this whole officer thing is as silly as you do. Me with six months, you with fifteen years . . . But it is the way it is.' Garvie nods. It is not quite mutual respect, at least on Garvie's side, but it is at least mutual understanding. This ability to manoeuvre almost outside of the class-inflected officer/rank hierarchies of the British Army marks out the SAS elite forces here as a separate and distinctive kind of soldier. That the distinction is not only one of class is also underlined by the fact that two members of Red Troop, the brothers Alex and Sam, are themselves upper class. This is highlighted in the Red Troop 'family meal' referred to above. The team are waiting to go in to action and have access to a hotel kitchen. They have prepared what can only be described as a banquet. Jem says: 'Sam, Alex – wine cellar's through there. With you being aristocratic I'm sure you'll know what to do.' He goes on, 'How come you and Sam aren't Ruperts? Being aristocratic and that.' Sam replies flippantly, 'Inverted snobbery.' It is not that they hide or deny their upper class identity, however. Sam, on pouring the wine, demonstrates his class credentials saying, with only a trace of irony. 'Should really have had time to breathe, but needs must.' But the others are just as capable of enjoying these aristocratic pleasures. Working class Jamie, on tasting the wine, immediately recognises its quality, exclaiming 'Jesus!' When the lights go out, the candlelit meal becomes an archetypal banquet image, with fine crockery and glassware, lighted candelabras, roast meats, platters of exotic fruit, including pineapples, and fine wines. This visually constructs an image of the Special Forces as the 'aristocracy' of the British Armed Forces.

In some ways this is also a utopian image of the diverse British armed forces that is the object of the early twenty-first century diversity policies discussed in Chapter 3: a team of men of different classes and colours – white, black, Asian, upper class, working class, English, Scots. They are cooking for each other, waiting on each other, pouring wine for each other. They are a team beyond race, beyond class, bonded as a 'family', but there not because they were born to it but because they have proven themselves worthy. The new member Jamie takes up his new place in this family as he is shown to the head of the table. Garvie, the father figure, tastes the wine. They are still all men of course, and all coded as heterosexual – this diversity only goes so far. Although there are significant female military figures associated with Red Troop as the series progresses, at this stage this iconic image is reserved for its bonded male family.

As noted in Chapter 4, the inculcation of loyalty to one's peers or 'mates' is a crucial part of the process of becoming an infantry soldier, and these bonds are coded as thoroughly masculine. The bonds between the soldiers in Red Troop are tangible in the series' many action scenes, in which they are shown working as a close unit, covering each other and relying on each other. The male bonding that holds Red Troop together goes beyond this mutual dependence in action, however. Their bonds are also constructed as having an emotional dimension, shown through a number of intimately shot scenes.

In episode one, for example, there is a scene between the two new members of the team, Alex and Jamie, as they are waiting to go into action for the first time. They are lying side by side on a double bed, contemplating their first military action, and talking about their fears. 'Which is it for you?' says Alex, 'Fear of killing or being killed?' 'Neither,' says Jamie. 'Just afraid of cocking things up . . . I needed to see if I was up to it.' 'Tomorrow we'll know.' Alex turns out the light. Darkness descends. Both characters are very still during this exchange, and the impression produced by this, the close-ups and the nature of their exchange, is that this is a moment of deep contemplation. Constructed in terms of intimacy – the bed, their implied physical closeness, the use of close-ups, and the sharing of anxieties – this is offered as an emotionally charged moment of closeness. Unlike the disturbing emotional ties and responsibilities that tie Jamie to his family, these male bonds are forged through shared experience. It is notable also how the construction of the scene works to control and close down the potential sexual associations of this shared moment, where both characters are lying on a double bed, quite literally about to go to sleep together. Alex and Jamie are never seen in the same shot; the camera alternates between them so they are kept in separate frames. Their bodies are not shown – only their faces in close-up – and they remain perfectly still, each looking ahead. Their bonding, the visual construction of the scene asserts, is homosocial.

The importance of this emotional openness between members of Red Troop is underlined in episode two, when there are tensions within the team. These come to a head in a scene between Alex and Jem, and are worked out through a combination of emotional intimacy and violence. Jem says, punching Alex, 'you want to bottle shit up inside, you're in the wrong outfit and the wrong regiment. You got shit to say, you say it. That's what we're here for. You can talk to me. I'm an approachable guy . . . Speak nice. Speak to me.' This is a highly charged exchange – emotional, intimate and violent at the same time. Their faces are only inches away from each other. Although the scene reinforces the notion that emotional openness between these men is desirable, it also puts it in its place as a private matter between men. Jem's closing joke is 'don't ever tell anybody I've got a heart. I'd have to kill you.'

These moments of emotional revelation and closeness almost always take place in private between two men. The bonds between the men as a group are drawn publicly in the action scenes and in the off-duty drinking scenes. Here, though, the tone is robust and jokey, rather than tender or close. When the men drink a toast to Sam who has been killed in action, they are briefly quiet, until Garvie mobilises them: 'Alright, that's enough', adding 'We're not Americans.' In public situations, then, the British soldier demonstrates a masculinity that eschews overtly sentimental or public displays of emotion. As a TV drama series, *Ultimate Force* reinforces this construction of the British soldier, while allowing a glimpse behind the scenes at his emotional landscape. Emotional openness, it suggests, has its place between soldiers but that place is in private. Unlike the emotional dimensions of the characters in *Soldier Soldier*, which are seen in their relationships with their wives and families, the emotional relationships in *Ultimate Force* are between the men of the Red Troop family.

The action scenes of *Ultimate Force* predictably celebrate those aspects of military masculinities that are related to the combat role. Garvie, for example, is shown to be capable of extreme violence. Some of his violence, perpetrated in the line of duty, is shown as quite brutal. For example, in one episode he strangles an enemy – an IRA hostage-taker. No quick gunshot – the death is relatively lengthy and shows Garvey using his brute strength to kill with his hands. In another scene he shoots a hostage-taker in an attempted bank robbery. This villain is a young boy, whose character had been quite sympathetically fleshed out through his relationship with a motherly woman hostage. He is cowering under the protection of this woman when Garvie shoots him at close range. Reporting back later, Garvie says crisply, 'He went for his weapon, I thought it constituted a threat and I duly fired.' This controlled violence and capacity for putting aside one's emotional response to violence is shown in episode one to be something that has to be inculcated in the soldier – that he has to both learn and find it in himself to do. This is shown through the figure of Jamie. On his first operation, in the first episode, he sees Sam shot, and has to remember his training, call in the shooting and move on rather than following the impulse to stop and help his mate. Garvie's masculinity is, at the same time, however, naturalised. This is suggested in a statement he makes in the pub, 'Human beings have to be taught to appreciate beauty, music, art, sculpture. Good manners. It all has to be taught. The only things that come natural are eating, fighting and shagging.' In the main, Garvie's masculinity is naturalised through his repeated construction as a 'natural leader'. For example, when being briefed by a Home Office official at one point, he steps in before his commanding officer to ask questions. The official asks, 'Captain, who's in charge here? You or the Sergeant?' Garvie responds crisply, 'Him', but his demeanour suggests otherwise. He is constructed as having a 'natural' authority, which is counterposed to the imposed authority of the 'inexperienced Ruperts', and also, for example, to that of the villain in episode one, who insists that his 'men' and his hostages call him 'Boss'. He constantly needs to reassert this, repeatedly saying 'call me Boss', because his assumption of authority is perverted and unnatural.

Ultimate Force, as television drama, offers a fantasy that celebrates the masculinities associated with the deployment of 'ultimate force' and the elite warrior image. It celebrates its characters' controlled violence, courage, toughness, stoicism and their male bonds, and asserts their heterosexual sexuality. This is also a fantasy of diverse British armed forces, echoing the policy discourses on diversity that were discussed in Chapter 3. In Red Troop it offers an image of a bonded team, working together across many axes of difference. It even goes so far, in series three, as to include a woman in that team.

In series three, the first episode, entitled 'Deadlier Than The Male' introduces the figure of Becca Gallagher as the first and only woman in the cohort of soldiers who are in the final stages of selection. The fact that a woman has made it so far through the selection process is causing some consternation to the officer Dempsey, and to Garvie who has been informed that if she gets through she is going into Red Troop. The narrative of the episode shows Becca getting through the training, being chosen by Garvie for a hijack operation for which the hijackers have asked for a female pilot, acquitting herself well in partnership with Garvie ('Cracking job', says Garvie approvingly) and gaining acceptance into Red Troop.

Several of the key moments in this narrative foreground Becca's body. When we are first introduced to her she is naked, taking her place in a row of naked male soldiers. Dempsey is telling Garvie 'One of them has breasts'. The camera moves to show Becca's naked body, breasts included, in the line of naked men. This is a highly ambiguous image. It is not overtly sexualised, as with the sexualised figures seen in the tabloids. Her female body just takes its place alongside the naked male bodies, and she proceeds to pull on her uniform just as they do. She appears unconcerned and unselfconscious about being naked, just as the men do. Later, in the interrogation part of the testing, she is naked again, just as the other soldiers have been stripped naked for interrogation. Garvie gives her the beret, the signal that she has got through selection. Finally, the scene that marks her acceptance into Red Troop is another naked scene, in which, following the successful operation, she enters the communal shower along with the male soldiers of Red and Blue Troops. One of them smirks, 'You wouldn't pick up my soap would you, love?' And she responds with a blow that knocks him to the ground. The others laugh with approval. Becca's nakedness in these scenes is highly ambiguous and double edged. On one level it is offered in a way that implies that her nakedness is just like the nakedness of the other male soldiers in selection or in the shower. It is routine, unremarkable and non-sexualised nakedness. It is presented in this way in terms of how it is shot and lit, her unconcerned attitude and body posture, and the gazes of the other characters in the scenes, none of which is coded as sexual. At the same time, of course, this female nakedness amidst the nakedness of male soldiers is not necessarily an unremarkable or asexualised image for the viewer. It foregrounds her sex difference – we are, after all, introduced to her via her breasts – and of course it provides plenty of opportunities for the audience to look at her naked body.

The discourse around the incorporation of this woman soldier is that there is a place for her in the team. She just has to prove herself, just as a man has to, and be tested. This follows the same logic as the gender-free physical testing discussed in Chapter 3, taking it to a logical conclusion. Once Becca has proved herself and been accepted into Red Troop, her gendered difference becomes just another axis of difference within the diverse team, and is relatively unremarked upon in subsequent episodes. The narrative implausibility of Becca's easy acceptance by Garvie and Red Troop, and the oddness and ambiguity of the naked scenes seem to underline the fact that this representation of the relatively easy inclusion of a woman SAS soldier is a fantasy – women still cannot do that job in 'real life' – and a fantasy that sits at odds with the generic requirements of the elite soldier narrative that it should claim to offer an accurate depiction of soldiering. The idea of accuracy had been provided in the first two series by the employment of ex-SAS soldier and author Chris Ryan as 'technical supervisor' on the series. Ryan had departed, along with a number of the regular cast, at the end of the second series. The third and fourth series of the programme were less popular, and popularly regarded as poor,[23] with the fourth series being taken off the air before its end. The series seems to break under the strain of its competing discourses: its celebration of the elite military masculinities of the Special Forces and its circulation of Army diversity discourse. It is possible that, combined with this, its fantasy of female integration, with its troubling implications, set up tensions from which it could not recover.

Conclusion

Figures of the soldier, both male and female, have circulated widely in British media and popular culture in recent years, and these figures are articulated differently at different times. For example, we can see a shift from *Soldier Soldier's* 1990s fascination with ordinary soldiers and the tensions of their everyday lives to *Ultimate Force*'s celebratory representations of elite soldiers in the early twenty-first century. This shift echoes the shifting context, from the 1990s repositioning of the armed forces as a peace-keeping and humanitarian force to the military engagements of the early twenty-first century.

At a time in the 1990s when the British Army is engaged in restructuring, having to re-imagine its role, and beginning further to integrate women into formerly male jobs, the figure of the female soldier becomes a potent representational figure, circulating widely in newspapers before finding herself at the centre of a prime time TV drama. It is worth noting that the appearance of the figure of the female soldier in media discourse is more numerous and significant than the actual numbers of female soldiers would suggest. The importance of the media figure of the female soldier lies not in her 'representativeness' but in her cultural resonance as a ground for the working out of shifting constructions of gender and ideas about gender roles. She is a figure that tests the limits of what women are and what they can do. This makes her potentially a transgressive figure that can trouble the norms of gender. As we have seen, the figure of the woman soldier is frequently contained by discourses around her sexuality, disruptiveness and limitations, and is subject to strategies that normalise her as properly feminine. But, we might ask, how compete is this containment? How hard do these news stories, images and fictional narratives have to work to contain the figure of the female soldier? Despite the kinds of containment that we have described, the image of the woman who is a soldier still has the potential to do symbolic damage to the figure of the soldier as male. That potential and that containment are never fixed, which is one of the reasons why the figure of the female soldier has been endlessly fascinating and recurring in popular culture.

As we have seen, there are many connections between these figures, the discourses they circulate and those that circulate through army policy, for example. Some connections are direct, as when there has been army institutional involvement in, or sanctioning of, TV series like *Red Cap*, which sometimes seems to function as an extension of Army PR and recruitment advertisements for the army as an equal opportunities employer. Some connections are less direct, as when both press and Army policy discourse circulate longstanding discourses on the feminine as disruptive, sexualised, limited or maternal. Soldiers read newspapers and watch TV drama series – in fact, scrutiny of Internet bulletin boards suggests that they are particularly fond of watching and commenting on military-themed TV series. These connections between military discourse and popular cultural discourse are not one-way or simple, but feed into each other.

6 The politics of gender and the contemporary British Army

We will conclude by returning to the two questions posed in our introduction. The first question was about how gender might work as an axis of difference within the British Army, and the consequences of this in terms of gender relations and identities within that institution. The second question was about how military and civilian understandings about gender, both within the Army and beyond, might intersect, and what this might mean for our wider understanding of military issues. In addressing these questions, we have argued around a small number of key observations; that women's participation is quite carefully contained within an institution that has always required labour from its civilian society; that ideas about female difference are ambivalent in outcome, sometimes overcome through activities designed to be gender fair and sometimes rendered problematic because of their difference from male norms; that discourses about women soldiers portray these soldiers as potentially disruptive and problematic, an idea that has purchase in both military and popular cultural representations; and that models of masculinity in the military value a specific embodied male military identity that structures men's military participation in certain specific ways, and also determines the subject positions available to women personnel. We have framed these observations within an argument that says, emphatically, that gender is a military issue, and that military gender issues are the proper concern of us all, wherever we are positioned in relation to the armed forces.

The imaginary army

Above all else, we have insisted that discourses – systems of ideas that give things meaning – are quite fundamental to all this. In doing so, we are emphasising the realm of the cultural, not as one of a number of variables such as 'the economy', 'the political system' or 'society', which can be used to investigate some sort of observable reality, but as a realm of material and discursive practices that are foundational to what we think that reality is. So, for example, we are arguing less for an appreciation of 'culture' as an explanatory factor in understanding, say, the balancing of power within relations between military institutions and their host societies (although, within the epistemological and ontological frameworks that structure much contemporary Anglophone military sociology, we would endorse the extension of academic inquiry to consider culture). Rather, we are arguing for an analytic approach to the military that sees knowledge about the military, by which we mean our ideas and understandings about that institution and its material conditions, as a reflection of discursive practices. Discourses are fundamental because they give meaning to a material reality, they make things 'real'. Discursive practices bring the Army into being; they are how we imagine the Army into existence.

This is not to somehow deny that the Army has a material reality – that is evident enough in the cold metal of the weapons systems it uses, the warm bodies of its troops, the physical presence of its bases, the tangible volume of its supplies of matériel. But the destructive power of those weapons systems, the resilience (or vulnerability) of those bodies, the security or permeability of those bases, the rationales for those supplies, we argue, are not intrinsic to those things, but are inscribed upon those things by discourses and discursive practice. The Army – as with any military institution – achieves its form and structure, its sense of what it is and what it does, through discourses. Discourses are a constant, dynamic process of imagination through which the Army's reason for existence (the deployment of armed force at the behest of the state), its structure (a hierarchy of command and obedience) and its ethos (selfless commitment, loyalty, discipline) all come into being. To put this another way, the rationale for, structure of and ethos of the Army are not entities that have an independent existence outside and beyond the ideas that bring them into being; they exist and are identifiable through that process of being brought into being. Furthermore, this is a constant, complex and infinitely repeated performance; it is that constant repetition of discursive practices that constitutes what we call 'the Army'.

These discursive processes that bring the Army into being, and which define the category 'army', also define 'civilian'. For either of these categories to make sense, they require the existence of the other. In many ways, they are each others' 'other', the thing that each defines itself in opposition to. This process of defining self in relation to 'other' is constantly negotiated; that process of definition is one through which meaning is made. As Stuart Hall puts it (while talking about the discursive practices around national identity): 'What it means to be "British" or "Russian" or "Jamaican" cannot be entirely controlled by the British, Russians, or Jamaicans, but is always up for grabs, always being negotiated, in the dialogue between these national cultures and their "others" '.[1]

We find it helpful, then, to think of civil–military relations not in terms of two observable entities linked and separated at strategic points, but as the outcome of discursive practice, a constantly evolving network of ideas through which the categories of 'civilian' and 'military' are constructed, and through which the materiality of armed forces are given meaning and brought into being. Furthermore, the role of civilian cultural practices is essential here; ideas that circulate in civilian culture, particularly, but not exclusively, in popular culture and media, are so important because they are part of that dialogue and negotiation through which our armed forces are given meaning. Arguably, they are the dominant forums for that negotiation in our mediated world.

We are aware, of course, that these ideas that we have just mapped out might be considered a little radical to some, even perhaps peculiar. We should note, however, the salience of these ideas of the significance of discursive practices in re-energising the study of international relations and geopolitics.[2] These emergent approaches to the study of the state, national identity and geopolitical relations have, we would argue, much to offer contemporary Anglophone military sociology by way of analytic and methodological example. We would also like to reiterate an argument that we made in the introduction – the act of studying and writing about the military is an act of academic citizenship and constructive engagement. A world without ideas about how ideas work is a dull but dangerous place.

The politics of gender in the contemporary British Army

One of the ways in which the Army is imagined or brought into being is through discourses on gender. As we have pointed out already, but will repeat for emphasis, discourses on gender are not the only discursive practices through which armed forces are made meaningful. They are, though, a significant and influential part of the mix.

The discursive practices, through which ideas about gender are constructed, articulated, negotiated and circulated, work by setting the boundaries of where men and women can be within military institutions. They define the places that men and women can occupy. They shape the possibilities of what an individual, a person, can be, on the basis of his or her biological sex. As we argued in Chapter 2, they operate (and have always done so) to contain women's military participation, to equate military participation with the male and the masculine, and have always constituted a space in which wider social norms of masculinity and femininity are worked out with reference to the differences between the categories 'military' and 'civilian'. As we argued in Chapter 3, discursive constructions of gender as an axis of difference that is (variously) contained, controlled for, negated or represented as a problem (depending on the issue at hand) are all part of the process through which the Army is brought into being as a masculine institution. As we argued in Chapter 4, the discursive practices through which the identity of the soldier is made are performed through activities that continually confirm that identity as male and as masculine. As we argued in Chapter 5, popular cultural forms such as print media and television drama consolidate those soldier identities from beyond the barrack gates through a range of discursive strategies.

The discursive construction of male military masculinities, this continual process of affirmation of the connections between the male body, military participation and attributes identified and valorised as masculine, has enormous consequences for the subject position of military women because it shapes the availability and nature of the positions that it is possible for those women to occupy. We do not deny that many women, the world over, enjoy productive and meaningful military lives; we have met some of them during the course of our research. What is striking, though, is the frequency with which the performance of male masculinities in some forms is reported as limiting for military women, in fashions that range from the vaguely annoying to the downright abusive. In a study of the progress of gender integration in the Canadian combat arms, for example, the first women participants were clear that they identified the real challenges of this occupational choice as the endurance of the rejection and bias against them, evident in both covert and overt attempts to remove them from the combat arms, rather than the challenges of the job itself.[3]

> The environment has been defined by men and maintained to train and employ men. The world that women enter is a world that defines and reinforces gender roles in a way that is in conflict with the role of a woman in the combat arms. Consequently, a woman's motivation to take on a 'male role' is suspect. Within the combat arms, the motivations and behaviours of each woman are interpreted in a way that leaves no room for women to be there because they 'want to do the job'. On the other hand, women understand that they will have to become 'one of the guys' if they are going to succeed. In the end, there is nowhere for them to go because they cannot achieve either of these conflicting roles.[4]

Another example, from Barrett's work on the US Navy, discusses this as well, identifying the three possible strategies for identity construction that women naval officers deploy in order to make a place for themselves: variously, masculinising strategies, playing the lady or being the degendered professional.[5] Professional identification is fundamentally difficult for these Navy women because of the limitations imposed by whatever strategy they choose. Katerina Agostino's research into women in the Royal Australian Navy echoes these findings; she talks of the strategies such as identification with masculine norms of behaviour or of the performance of sexualised or ultrafeminine femininities.[6] Some find coping strategies. Others are forced out. Leah Mates, a corporal originally from the Royal Signals, made British newspaper headlines in 2005 following the award to her of damages for sexual discrimination, following an employment tribunal that heard evidence of a range of sexually harassing incidents. In her statement to the tribunal, she said of these incidents that she 'now began to understand that the Army is a male preserve and a woman who tries to establish herself does so at the peril of her health and happiness'.[7] We can add that the construction of male military masculinities is not without problems for men either; some men are beneficiaries but others are not.

The discursive practices through which armed forces are given meaning are political. They are political because in defining the parameters through which gender identities are performed and negotiated, and through which gender relations are understood, they become the mechanism through which power operates and relationships of domination and subordination are consolidated. The most trenchant of the discursive practices around gender, its power reflected in its dominance and consistency, is that which equates the military with the masculine in such a way as to render that relationship natural, and intractable or inextricable because of this. This relationship is only 'natural' because it has become naturalised, the outcome of consistent efforts made to sustain that connection or forge that link. The discursive strategies that naturalise the connection between masculinities and armed conflict are a mechanism through which military identity (whether individual or collective) is performed, part of the process through which armed forces are imagined, brought into being, made meaningful.

An outcome of this discourse of naturalisation is the legitimation of uncontrolled male behaviour, behaviour that is represented as potentially uncontrollable because it originates within essentialised notions of masculinity as wild and uncontrolled. Consider, for example, the following statement: 'The MoD recognises that the majority of recruits and those responsible for their training are male and that this might give rise to inappropriate behaviour towards women during training.'[8]

Our reading of this statement is that it implies that men might behave inappropriately towards women, because they are men. Interestingly, it is taken from one of the measures (on gender balance in training) within the Ministry of Defence (MoD) and Equal Opportunities Commission (EOC) action plan on addressing sexual harassment. The potential for uncontrolled male behaviour would appear to be recognised within the core of the MoD's considerable efforts to eradicate (or at least limit) sexual harassment within the armed forces. Indeed, one of the activities agreed between the MoD and EOC has been the commissioning of research specifically amongst men, in order to understand why harassment occurs, what could be done to prevent and deal with it, and how awareness and commitment to change might be developed.[9]

This idea of the uncontrollable male soldier is as problematic as that of the naturally disruptive woman. This idea, in some ways, is part of the discursive figure of the 'squaddie', a figure that has currency in British military and popular culture, and is constituted within and outside the military. Variously portrayed as one of 'Our Boys', or a loveable rogue, or a derided and marginalised figure because of his transgressions, or a brutalised victim of a brutal military culture, the squaddie is always configured as potentially uncontrollable and potentially resistant to the discipline of the Army. Indeed, as we said in Chapter 4, practices around 'letting go' could be explained as a safety valve, a respite, a form of temporary resistance to the regulation of behaviour in Army life.

This is a significant point, because the essentialising of uncontrolled male behaviours as a naturalised feature of some military masculinities (particularly but not exclusively those associated with the infantry) speaks directly to and is intimately connected to discourses about violence and its legitimacy. These discourses on violence are quite fundamental to the ways in which the armed forces are understood, given meaning. Armed forces, as we have said, come into being and are constituted, in terms of their meaning, through discursive practices. This book has been written at a particular historical moment at which the tensions within discourses on violence are being worked through, often very painfully. It would seem appropriate therefore to engage with this issue.

Soldiers kill and injure; they are granted legitimacy to do so by the state, sanctioned through the rules of engagement. Their abilities to do so are trained into them.

> Well, with Guardsmen, you have to train them for an aggressive eventuality. At the end of the day they're the ones that's going actually to go in and kill the enemy, so they've got to have a little bit of physical robustness as well as a bit of aggression as well – once they hit the pain barrier then they start to get annoyed, you hear all the grunts and groans and aggression coming out, and that's what they're basically looking for, in an Infantryman anyway.[10]

Soldiers use legitimate violence; that is what defines them as soldiers. What is critical at the present time are the ways in which the figure of the controlled or uncontrolled male is being drawn on within debates about the legitimacy of violence. Specifically, those debates – evidence of tensions at the heart of discourses on violence – are about the location of the boundaries between legitimate and illegitimate violence, the causes and consequences of controlled and uncontrolled military behaviour and, as part of this, the behaviours of the controlled or uncontrollable male.

These behaviours, placed in the public domain thanks to the prevalence of mobile digital recording and transmission technologies – mobile phones, hand-held moving image recorders, digital cameras – include incidents such as the assault on Iraqi civilians at Camp Breadbasket, near Basrah in Iraq in May 2003, or the assault on a small group of Iraqi teenagers in Amara, Iraq in 2004. They also include incidents such as initiation rituals, training practices and disciplinary procedures. The differences of opinion articulated across the print and broadcast media, and on Internet discussion sites, show how unstable those boundaries are between legitimate and illegitimate violence, controlled and uncontrolled behaviour. Are the soldiers in Iraq brutal abusers or themselves the outcome of a system that has brutalised them to the extent that they are somehow unaware of the meanings of their actions? Are these men a few bad apples in an otherwise unblemished barrelful? Are their actions a legitimate expression of 'letting go', a necessary release from the pressures all soldiers must feel when they are involved in armed conflict? Are initiation rituals sadistic and brutal, or harmless and consensual, necessary and transformational? The politics of gender in the contemporary British Army are as much about the politics around the deployment of violence as they are around what men and women do as soldiers.

On the need for informed understanding

As we observed in Chapter 4, recent or substantial ethnographic research on the contemporary British Army is thin on the ground. As researchers, we have found this significant because it signals a gap in the research-based evidence base that has implications for how we have interpreted some of the practices we discuss. We want to close by reflecting on a parallel gap around wider social knowledge of the Army and armed forces. Popular cultural representations of the soldier, whether in print and broadcast media or through film and television drama, through military memoirs or websites, are significant for social understandings of the Army in the absence of wider social and personal experiences and contacts with the armed forces. The size of the armed forces as a proportion of the UK population is small; we have about 200,000 trained full-time military service personnel, to a UK population of about 60 million. Social knowledge of the armed forces is increasingly mediated through popular cultural forms. These mediate the military voices that we hear; what we hear are the voices of those able or wanting to write, or to broadcast, or to comment. This, in turn, means that there are other subject positions that exist but which, at a social level, we know little about.

This is not just a comment about the power of media forms to influence the discourses that circulate around the figures of the soldier. There is a wider moral point here too, about the need for social (as well as political and military) engagement with the military covenant that exists between soldier and society, and the need for the exchange of ideas between the two that consolidates that link.[11] As a society, we expect our armed forces to undertake specific tasks and perform specific roles. It is remarkable how little we know about these people, given what we ask them to do.

Notes

1 Gender and the British Army

1 Debates about the sex/gender distinction, drawing on the work of Butler and Gatens, point to the complexities around the conceptualisation of both terms, arguing that both sex and gender can be understood as constructed rather than essential categories, complicit with each other. We do not talk into these debates here, but readers should note the instability of these terms. See J. Butler, *Bodies That Matter: On the Discursive Limits of 'Sex'*, London: Routledge, 1994; M. Gatens, *Imaginary Bodies: Ethics, Power and Corporeality*, London: Indiana University Press, 1996.

2 Although we use the terms 'military' and 'armed forces' interchangeably here, we should note the subtleties of variation in the use of these terms in different forms of the English language. British English conventionally refers to 'armed forces' or 'armed services' when referring to that institution charged by the state with the deployment of armed violence, and the British Armed Forces as the collective proper noun to refer to its three constitutive branches – the Army, the Royal Navy and the Royal Air Force. North American English refers more usually to 'the military' rather than 'armed forces'.

3 We should emphasise here that the issues around relations between militaries and the state, and between armed forces and civil society, are complex and raise a number of challenges around the democratic governance of armed forces, at levels from the macro to the micro, which we do not consider in this book. For a comprehensive and authoritative discussion of civil–military relations in contemporary Europe, see A. Forster, *Armed Forces and Society in Europe*, London: Palgrave Macmillan, 2005.

4 Note, however, that within contemporary political science debates about security and defence there is recognition of the increasingly fragmented relationship between the state and the deployment of legitimate violence. Jabri, for example, argues that contemporary practices of global war can be more accurately understood as a matrix of state and non-state actors, where violence targets communities and individuals as well as states. V. Jabri, 'War, security and the liberal state', *Security Dialogue* 37 (1), 2006, pp. 47–64.

5 For a good introduction to the vast literature on gender and armed conflict, and women and war, see: L. A. Lorentzen, and J. Turpin (eds), *The Women and War Reader*, New York: New York University Press, 1998; C. Enloe, *Maneuvres: The International Politics of Militarizing Women's Lives*, Berkeley, CA: University of California Press, 2000; S. Jacobs, R. Jacobson and J. Marchbank (eds), *States of Conflict: Gender, Violence and Resistance*, London: Zed Books, 2000; C. Moser and F. Clark (eds), *Victims, Perpetrators or Actors? Gender, Armed Conflict and Political Violence*, New York: Zed Books, 2001.

6 Also worth noting at this point is the relative lack of studies of the military in general

(gender orientated or otherwise) in British social science and cultural studies, in comparison with the wealth of research and scholarship in political science and international relations, on the outcomes and consequences of military action. With notable exceptions – see, for example, the work of Christopher Dandeker, Martin Shaw, Paul Higate, David Morgan, Anthony Forster, Victoria Basham and Tony King – British social science has not pursued academic research agendas around the sociology and culture of the military with the same vigour observable in, for example, the USA, Canada, Germany, the Netherlands and Slovenia. For commentary on British military sociology, see C. Dandeker, 'Armed Forces and society research in the United Kingdom: a review of British military sociology', in G. Kümmel and A. G. Prüfert (eds), *Military Sociology: The Richness of a Discipline*, Baden-Baden: Nomos, 2000, pp. 68–90. Similarly, contemporary Anglophone human geography, despite the military origins of the discipline and the significance of armed conflict in shaping space and place, has been reluctant to engage with the military as a geographical institution. See R. Woodward, *Military Geographies*, Oxford: Blackwell, 2004; R. Woodward, 'From Military Geographies to militarism's geographies: disciplinary engagements with the geographies of militarism and military activities', *Progress in Human Geography* 29 (6), 2005, pp. 718–740.

7 For examples of cross-comparative work, see Charles Moskos and colleagues' use of gender within their 'postmodern military' thesis (C. Moskos, J. A. Williams and D. R. Segal (eds), *The Postmodern Military: Armed Forces After the Cold War*, Oxford: Oxford University Press, 2000), Mady Wechsler Segal and colleagues' cross-national comparative work modelling predictive factors around women's military participation (M. W. Segal, 'Women's military roles cross-nationally: past, present and future'. *Armed Forces and Society* 9 (6), 1995, pp. 757–775; and S. Trainor, M. Leithauser and M. W. Segal, 'Women's participation in armed forces cross-nationally: expanding Segal's model', *Current Sociology* 50 (5), 2002, pp. 771–797) and Joshua Goldstein's transhistorical, transnational survey of the gendering of warfare (J. Goldstein, *War and Gender: How Gender Shapes the War System and Vice Versa*, Cambridge: Cambridge University Press, 2001).

8 For a wider discussion and analysis of social difference in the contemporary British Armed Forces, see V. Basham (2006) *An Analysis of Social Diversity in the British Armed Forces*, unpublished PhD thesis, Department of Politics, University of Bristol.

9 There remains ample scope for comparative research in the differences and similarities between the three branches of the British Armed Forces with regard to gender issues, as there is little scholarly literature (that we can find) on this. The most up-to-date source is C. Dandeker, and M. W. Segal, 'Gender integration in the Armed Forces: recent policy developments in the United Kingdom', *Armed Forces & Society* 23 (1), 1996, pp. 29–47.

10 R. Smith, *The Utility of Force: The Art of War in the Modern World*, Harmondsworth: Penguin, 2006.

11 That said, there are interesting questions about the degree to which secrecy is politically rather than operationally necessary; for a popular interpretation about the 'need' for secrecy, written by a former member of the armed forces, see L. Page, *Lions, Donkeys and Dinosaurs: Waste and Blundering in the Armed Forces*, London: Heineman, 2006. For an academic view, see G. Kümmel, 'When boy meets girl: the "feminization" of the military: an introduction also to be read as a post-script', *Current Sociology* 50 (5), 2002, pp. 615–639.

12 D. K. Thussu and D. Freedman (eds), 'Introduction', *Reporting Conflict 24/7*, London: Sage, 2003, pp. 1–12.

13 Adult Learning Inspectorate, *Safer Training: Managing Risks for the Welfare of Recruits in the British Armed Services*, Coventry: ALI, 2005.

14 M. MacDonald, *Exploring Media Discourse*, London: Arnold, 2003.

15 Our own experience is indicative here: a press release we put out in February 2003 summarising the research findings from an ESRC-funded research project on gender and the Army generated much higher levels of news coverage than is usual for the reporting of academic social scientific research.
16 See, for example, Maggie Magor's analysis of the gender politics around media reporting of the attacks in the United States in September 2001: M. Magor, 'News terrorism: misogyny exposed and the easy journalism of conflict', *Feminist Media Studies* 12 (1), 2002, pp. 141–144.
17 C. Nantais and M. Lee, 'Women in the US Military: protectors or protected? The case of prisoner of war Melissa Rathbun-Nealy', *Journal of Gender Studies* 8 (2), 1999, pp. 181–191.
18 On the discrepancy in the treatment of male and female sole parents in the US military, see M. Harris, 'Recognizing the role of women in NATO's military forces', *NATO Review* 45 (5), 197, pp. 25–26.
19 K. Muir, *Arms and the Woman*, London: Coronet, 1993. The film *Courage Under Fire* (1996), about the circumstances surrounding the death in action of a medical evacuation helicopter pilot, engaged precisely with these issues, the pilot in question being a mother who had died, leaving a young daughter orphaned.
20 For example, see S. Gutmann, *The Kinder, Gentler Military: Can America's Gender-Neutral Fighting Force Still Win Wars?* New York: Scribner, 2000; M. van Creveld, 'Less than we can be: men, women and the modern military', *Journal of Strategic Studies* 23 (4), 2000, pp. 1–20; M. van Creveld, *Men, Women and War*, London: Cassell, 2001.
21 Paul Higate and Ailsa Cameron highlight the dominance of what they call an 'engineering' rather than 'enlightenment' model of sociology in military sociology, for example. P. Higate, and A. Cameron, 'Reflexivity and researching the military', *Armed Forces & Society* 32 (2), 2006, pp. 219–233.
22 Joshua Goldstein's *Gender and War* (op. cit.) is recommended for its overview of theoretical approaches to the gender/military question, as is Katerina Agostino's (2000) 'Women in uniform: challenging feminisms', in K. Spurling, and E. Greenhalgh (eds), *Women in Uniform: Perceptions and Pathways*, ADFA, Canberra, 2000, pp. 64–82.
23 S. Whitworth, *Men, Militarism and UN Peacekeeping: A Gendered Analysis*, Boulder, CO: Lynne Rienner, 2004, p. 26.
24 Ibid, p.26
25 Ibid, p. 27.
26 Economic and Social Research Council project ref: R000223562, 'Gendered bodies, personnel policies and the culture of the British Army', Rachel Woodward and Trish Winter, 2001–2.

2 Patterns and histories of gender in the British Army

1 For an authoritative historical overview of the development of the British Army, useful reference sources are D. Chandler and I. Beckett, *The Oxford History of the British Army*, Oxford: Oxford University Press, 1996; R. Holmes (ed.), *The Oxford Companion to Military History*, Oxford: Oxford University Press, 2001.
2 All figures unless otherwise stated are from the Defence Analytical Services Agency (DASA) and are for April 2006, the most up-to-date data available at the time of writing.
3 Ministry of Defence (2006) *Women in the Armed Forces*, Public Information factsheet. Available at: http://www.mod.uk/DefenceInternet/FactSheets/WomenInTheArmedForces.htm, accessed 17 August 2006.
4 DASA statistics for 2006 show about 500 fewer women in total than the statistics used on the MoD website. In a group of 8,000 that is approximately a 6 per cent difference.

5 The distinction drawn between officers and 'other ranks', reflecting the hierarchical structure of armed forces everywhere, is one used by DASA for much of its data on armed forces personnel. For the British Armed Forces, socioeconomic class distinctions have historically mapped quite closely onto the commissioned officer/enlisted other ranks distinction. Although there are suggestions from von Zugbach and Ishaq that the officer class is becoming less elite in the British Armed Forces, popular accounts such as Paxman's and more abstract conceptually orientated investigations such as MacDonald's suggest that these class differences are entrenched and enduring. See R. von Zugbach and M. Ishaq, *Public Schools and Officer Recruitment in the British Army of the Late 20th Century*, University of Paisley, Working Paper, 1999; J. Paxman, *Friends in High Places: Who Runs Britain?*, Harmondsworth: Penguin, 1991, chapter 9; K. MacDonald, 'Black mafia, loggies and going for the stars: the military elite revisited', *Sociological Review* 52 (1), 2004, pp. 106–135.

6 The authoritative comparative work here is by Mady Wechsler Segal and colleagues: M. W. Segal, 'Women's military roles cross-nationally: past, present and future', *Armed Forces and Society* 9 (6), 1995, pp. 757–775, and the later reworking of this model in D. Iskra, S. Trainor, M. Leithauser and M. W. Segal, 'Women's participation in armed forces cross-nationally: expanding Segal's model', *Current Sociology* 50 (5), 2002, pp. 771–797.

7 NATO (2006) *Committee on Women in the NATO Forces, Country Reports*. Available at: http://www.nato.int/issues/women_nato/index.html, accessed 30 October 2006. For a detailed discussion of the US military, see L. Manning and V. R. Wright, *Women in the Military: Where they Stand*, 4th edn, Washington DC: Women's Research and Education Institute, 2002. For information on Canada, see D. Winslow and J. Dunn, 'Women in the Canadian Forces: between legal and social integration', *Current Sociology* 50 (5), 2002, pp. 641–667.

8 Department of Defence (2005) *Women in the Australian Defence Force*. Australian Government website: www.defence.gov.au/equity/women.htm, accessed 28 February 2005. For a discussion of the participation of women in the Royal Australian Navy, see K. Spurling, 'From exclusion to submarines: the integration of Australian women naval volunteers', *Australian Defence Force Journal* 139 (November/December), 1999, pp. 34–40; K. Agostino, 'Masculinity, sexuality and life on board Her Majesty's Royal Australian ships', *Journal of Interdisciplinary Gender Studies* 2 (1), 1997, pp. 15–30; K. Agostino, ' "She's a good hand": Navy women's strategies in masculinist workplaces', *Journal of Interdisciplinary Gender Studies* 3 (1), 1998, pp. 1–22.

9 L. Heinecken, 'Affirming gender equality: the challenges facing the South African armed forces', *Current Sociology* 50 (5), 2002, pp. 715–728.

10 Iskra *et al.*, 2002, op. cit.

11 Ibid. p. 779.

12 D.-S. Hong, 'Women in the South Korean Military', *Current Sociology* 50 (5), 2002, pp. 729–743.

13 Committee on Women in the NATO Forces (2006) *France* National Briefings and reports. Available at: http://www.nato.int/ims/2006/win/pdf/france_national_report%202006.pdf, accessed 30 October 2006.

14 There are exemptions for various categories of women and for some men, relating to citizenship, religious affiliation and ethnicity.

15 For a discussion of the Portuguese case, see H. Carreiras, 'Women in the Portuguese Armed Forces: from visibility to "eclipse" ', *Current Sociology* 50 (5), 2002, pp. 687–714.

16 Committee on Women in the NATO Forces (2006) *United States*. National Briefings and reports. Available at: http://www.nato.int/ims/2006/win/pdf/us_brief.pdf, accessed 11 November 2006.

17 G. Kümmel, 'Complete access: women in the Bundeswehr and male ambivalence', *Armed Forces & Society* 28 (4), 2002, pp. 555–573.

18 D. Pfarr, *Women in the Austrian Armed Forces*, Minerva: Quarterly Report on Women and the Military, Fall/Winter 1999.

19 L. Sion, ' "Too Sweet and Innocent for War"? Dutch peacekeepers and the use of violence', *Armed Forces & Society* 32 (3), 2006, pp. 454–474.

20 The French military's gendered history to 1990 is explored in J. Boulègue, ' "Feminization" and the French military: an anthropological approach', *Armed Forces & Society* 17 (3), 1991, pp. 343–363. For some background on the German armed forces, see Kümmel, 2002, op. cit.

21 L. Heinecken, 'Affirming gender equality: the challenges facing the South African armed forces', *Current Sociology* 50 (5), 2002, pp. 715–728.

22 Iskra *et al.*, 2002, op. cit.

23 U. Klein, 'The gender perspective of civil–military relations in Israeli society', *Current Sociology* 50 (5), 2002, pp. 669–686; U. Klein, ' "Our best boys": the gendered nature of civil–military relations in Israel', *Men and Masculinities* 2 (1), 1999, pp. 47–65; Y. Dar and S. Kimhi, 'Youth in the military: gendered experiences in the conscript service in the Israeli Army', *Armed Forces & Society* 30 (3), 2004, pp. 433–459; J. Robbins and U. Ben-Eliezer, 'New roles or "New Times"? Gender inequality and militarism in Israel's Nation-in-Arms', *Social Politics* 7 (3), 2000, pp. 309–342; O. Sasson-Levy, 'Constructing identities at the margins: masculinities and citizenship in the Israeli army', *Sociological Quarterly* 43, 2002, pp. 357–383; O. Sasson-Levy, 'Feminism and military gender practices: Israeli women soldiers in "masculine" roles', *Sociological Inquiry* 73, pp. 440–465; O. Sasson-Levy, 'Military, masculinity and citizenship: Tensions and contradictions in the experience of blue-collar soldiers', *Identities: Global Studies in Culture and Power* 10, 2003, pp. 319–345.

24 See, for example, B. Mitchell, *Women in the Military: Flirting with Disaster*, Washington DC: Regnery Publishing, 1999; M. van Creveld, 'Less than we can be: men, women and the modern military', *Journal of Strategic Studies* 23 (4), 2000, pp. 1–20; A. Gat, 'Female participation in war: biocultural interactions', *Journal of Strategic Studies* 23 (4), 2000, pp. 21–31; G. Frost, *Not Fit to Fight: The Cultural Subversion of the Armed Forces in Britain and America*, London: Social Affairs Unit, 1998.

25 For a good discussion of radical/difference feminist thought on women's military participation, see K. Agostino, 'Women in uniform: challenging feminisms', in K. Spurling and E. Greenhalgh (eds), *Women in Uniform: Perceptions and Pathways*, Canberra: ADFA, 2000, pp. 64–82.

26 C. Enloe, *Maneuvres: The International Politics of Militarizing Women's Lives*, Berkeley, CA: University of California Press, 2000.

27 Agostino, 2000, op. cit. p. 73.

28 Agostino, 2000, op. cit. p. 73.

29 L. M. Miller, 'Feminism and the exclusion of Army women from combat', *Gender Issues* 16 (3), 1998, pp. 33–64.

30 R. Titunik, 'The first wave: gender, integration and military culture', *Armed Forces & Society* 26 (2), 2000, pp. 229–257.

31 R. W. Connell, 'Masculinity, violence and war', in P. Patton and R. Poole (eds), *War/Masculinity*, Sydney: Intervention, 1985.

32 J. Goldstein, *War and Gender: How Gender Shapes the War System and Vice Versa.* Cambridge: Cambridge University Press, 2001, p. 9.

33 L. Noakes, *Women in the British Army: War and the Gentle Sex, 1907–1948*, London: Routledge, 2006.

34 B. D. Porter, *War and the Rise of the State*, New York: Free Press, 1994; A. Giddens, *The Nation-State and Violence*, Berkeley, CA, University of California Press, 1987; M. Mann, *The Sources of Social Power*, Cambridge: Cambridge University Press, 1986.

35 D. French, *Military Identities: The Regimental System, the British Army and the British People, 1870–2000* Oxford: Oxford University Press, 2006.

36 For a discussion of this, see B. Crim, 'Silent partners: women and warfare in Early Modern Europe', in G. J. DeGroot and C. Peniston-Bird (eds), *A Soldier and a Woman: Sexual Integration in the Military*, Harlow: Longman, 2000, pp. 18–32.

37 S. N. Hendrix, 'In the Army: women, camp followers and gender roles in the British Army in the French and Indian Wars, 1755–1765', in G. J. DeGroot, C. Peniston-Bird, C. (eds), *A Soldier and a Woman: Sexual Integration in the Military*, Harlow: Longman, 2000, pp. 33–48. For a discussion of the American military and its camp followers, see B. S. Alt and B. S. Stone, *Campfollowing: A History of the Military Wife*, New York: Praeger, 1991.

38 See, for example, Kate Adie's popular history of women and war, a book based around a major Imperial War Museum exhibition in 2003. K. Adie, *Corsets to Camouflage: Women and War*, London: Hodder & Stoughton, 2003.

39 R. Kipling, *The Complete Barrack Room Ballads of Rudyard Kipling*, C. Carrington (ed.). London: Methuen, 1973.

40 C. Schmitz, 'We too were soldiers': the experiences of British nurses in the Anglo-Boer War, 1899–1902', in G. J. DeGroot and C. Peniston-Bird (eds), *A Soldier and a Woman: Sexual Integration in the Military*, Harlow: Longman, 2000, pp. 49–62.

41 For a detailed history, see Noakes, 2006, op. cit.

42 J. Robinson, *Mary Seacole*, London: Constable and Robinson, 2006.

43 See, for example, R. Pennington and R. Higham, *Amazons to Fighter Pilots: A Biographical Dictionary of Military Women*, Westport, CT: Greenwood Press, 2003; J. Wheelwright, *Amazons and Military Maids: Women who Dressed as Men in the Pursuit of Life, Liberty and Happiness*, London: Pandora Press, 1989.

44 D. J. Oddy, 'Gone for a soldier: the anatomy of a nineteenth-century army family'. *Journal of Family History* 25 (1), 2000, pp. 39–62. Oddy constructs a fascinating account of subsequent generations of a Scottish military family, at a time when the options for accompanied and institutionally supported service were minimal.

45 Noakes, 2006, op. cit. See also G. Dawson, *Soldier Heroes: British Adventure, Empire and the Imagining of Masculinity*, London: Routledge, 1994; M. Paris, *Warrior Nation: Images of War in British Popular Culture 1850–2000*, London: Reaktion Books, 2000.

46 Noakes, 2006, op. cit. Additional sources on women's military participation from the founding of WAAC include: S. Bidwell, *The Women's Royal Army Corps*, London: Leo Cooper, 1977; T. Roy, *Women in Khaki: The Story of the British Woman Soldier*, London: Columbus Books, 1988.

47 Quoted in Bidwell, 1977, op. cit., p. 1.

48 See Noakes, 2006, op. cit.; M. Higonnet, J. Jenson, S. Michel and M. C. Weitz (eds), *Behind the Lines: Gender and the Two World Wars*. Whitehaven, MD: Yale University Press, 1987; M. Higonnet, *Nurses at the Front: Writing the Wounds of the Great War*, New Haven, CT: Northeastern University Press, 2001; G. Braybon and P. Summerfield, *Out of the Cage: Women's Experiences in Two World Wars*, London: Pandora Publishing, 1987. For a commentary on the historiography of the British, German and French experiences of gender change, see J. Winter and A. Prost, *The Great War in History: Debates and Controversies, 1914 to the Present*, Cambridge: Cambridge University Press, 2005, pp. 166–168.

49 Noakes, 2006, op. cit. p. 17.

50 N. Gullace, *The Blood of Our Sons: Men, Women and the Renegotiation of British Citizenship during the First World War*, London: Palgrave Macmillan, 2002.

51 For a discussion of the relationships between different strands of feminist thought and citizenship issues, primarily in the US context, see I. R. Feinman, *Citizenship Rites: Feminist Soldiers and Feminist Antimilitarists*, New York: New York University Press, 2000.

52 M. Siegel, ' "To the Unknown Mother of the Unknown Soldier": pacifism, feminism and the politics of sexual difference among French *Institutrices* between the Wars',

French Historical Studies 22(3), 1999, pp. 421–451; J. Vellacott, 'A place for pacifism and transnationalism in feminist theory: the early work of the Women's International League for Peace and Freedom', *Women's History Review* 2 (1), 1993, pp. 23–56; V. Woolf, *Three Guineas*, Harmondsworth: Penguin, 1997 [1938].

53 J. Bourke, *Dismembering the Male: Men's Bodies, Britain and the Great War*, London: Reaktion Books, 1996.

54 For a commentary on the rationales behind the use of aerial bombing campaigns, see S. Linquist, *A History of Bombing*, London: Granta Books, 2001.

55 Noakes, 2006, op. cit.

56 Noakes, 2006, op. cit., p. 120.

57 For a discussion of the gender dynamics of the German experience of the Second World War, see K. Hagemann and S. Schüler-Springorum (eds), *Home/Front: The Military, War and Gender in Twentieth Century Germany*, Oxford: Berg, 2000.

58 P. Summerfield and C. Peniston-Bird, 'Women in the firing line: the Home Guard and the defence of gender boundaries in Britain in the Second World War', *Women's History Review* 9, 2000, pp. 231–255.

59 Noakes, 2006, op. cit.

60 M. Gillies, *Waiting for Hitler: Voices from Britain on the Brink of Invasion*, London: Hodder & Stoughton, 2006.

61 Sources here are: B. S. Johnson, *All Bull: The National Servicemen*, London: Allison and Busby, 1973; T. Royle, *The Best Years of their Lives: The National Service Experience, 1945–1963*, London: Michael Joseph, 1986; T. Thorne, *Brasso, Blanco and Bull*, London: Constable and Robinson, 2000; T. Hickman, *The Call-Up: A History of National Service*, London: Headline, 2004.

62 D. Morgan, *It Will Make a Man of You: Notes on National Service, Masculinity and Autobiography*, Studies in Sexual Politics, University of Manchester, 1987.

63 Hickman, 2004, op. cit.

64 This applies to both our respective families; our fathers (Bob Winter and David Woodward) both 'got some in'.

65 For further information on the history and roles of the WRAC, see Noakes, 2006, op. cit.; Adie, 2003, op. cit; T. Roy, *Women in Khaki: The Story of the British Woman Soldier*, London: Columbus, 1988; C. Dandeker and M. W. Segal, 'Gender integration in Armed Forces: recent policy developments in the United Kingdom', *Armed Forces & Society* 23 (1), 1996, pp. 29–47.

66 Quoted in Adie, 2003, op. cit., p. 215.

67 C. Fowler, 'Integration of women into the Armed Services of the UK', in K. Spurling and E. Greenhalgh (eds), *Women in Uniform: Perceptions and Pathways*, UNSW at ADFA, Canberra, 2000, pp. 141–151.

68 L. Noakes, *War and the British: Gender, Memory and National Identity*, London: I. B. Tauris, 1998; K. Foster, *Fighting Fictions: War, Narrative and National Identity*, London: Pluto Press, 1999.

69 Dandeker and Segal, 1996, op. cit., K. Muir, *Arms and the Woman*, London: Coronet, 1993.

70 Noakes, 1998, op. cit., p.165.

71 See Muir, 1993, op. cit.

72 P. Bracken, 'Women in the Army', in H. Strachan (ed.), *The British Army: Manpower and Society into the Twenty-First Century*, London: Frank Cass, 2000.

73 MARILYN is an acronym for the 1989 Ministry of Defence report on Manning and Recruitment in the Lean Years of the Nineties. See M. Ridge, 'UK Military Manpower and Substitutability', *Defence Economics* 2, 1991, pp. 283–293.

74 See, for example, C. Dandeker and A. Strachan, 'Soldier recruitment in the British Army: a spatial and social methodology for analysis and monitoring', *Armed Forces & Society* 19 (2), 1993, pp. 279–290; A. Beevor, 'The implications of social change on the British Army', *British Army Review* 104, 1993, pp. 14–22.

75 C. Dandeker, 'Armed Forces and society research in the UK: a review of British military sociology', in G. Kümmel and A. D. Prüfert (eds), *Military Sociology: The Richness of a Discipline*, Baden-Baden: Nomos Verlag, 2000, pp. 68–90.
76 See Chapter 3, footnote 24, for literature on racism and ethnicity in the British armed forces.
77 See Chapter 3, footnote 1, for references to the literature on family policy and military wives.
78 For a discussion of the arguments around women's participation in military peacekeeping operations, see G. J. Degroot, 'A few good women: gender stereotypes, the military and peacekeeping', *International Peacekeeping* 8 (2), 2001, pp. 23–38. For a wider discussion of the gendered dimensions of peacekeeping, particularly masculinities, see S. Whitworth, *Men, Militarism and UN Peacekeeping: A Gendered Analysis*, Boulder, CO: Lynne Rienner, 2004; D. E. Mazurana, A. Raven-Roberts and J. L. Parpart, *Gender, Conflict, and Peacekeeping*, Lanham, MD: Rowman & Littlefield, 2005.
79 MoD, 2006, op. cit.
80 G. Frost, 'How to destroy an army', in G. Frost (ed.), *Not Fit to Fight: The Cultural Subversion of the Armed Forces in Britain and America*, London: Social Affairs Unit, 1998.
81 L. Page, *Lions, Donkeys and Dinosaurs: Waste and Blundering in the Armed Forces*, London: Heineman, 2006.
82 Segal, 1995, op. cit.
83 MoD, 2006, op. cit.

3 British Army personnel policies and the politics of female difference

1 We would like to thank Ann Murphy for sharing with us her thoughts, experiences, theories and data from her own research. See A. Murphy, *Is it 'Trouble and Strive' for the British Army Wife? A Study of their Thoughts and Opinions Regarding Identity and Current Access to Support Offered by the Ministry of Defence*, unpublished MA dissertation, School of Geography Politics and Sociology, Newcastle University. At the time of writing, research on Army wives is also ongoing at King's College University of London, but is still at the pre-publication stage. For research on fatherhood and its impact on military practice in a British context, see M. R. Osman, 'Fatherhood impacts on decision-making in conflict', *Defence Studies* 3, 2003, pp. 63–86. For a wider conceptualisation of family/military relationships, see M. W. Segal, 'The military and the family as greedy institutions', *Armed Forces & Society* 13, 1986, pp. 9–38; L. Laliberte and D. Harrison, *No Life Like It: Military Wives in Canada*, Toronto: J. Lorimer, 1994; M. C. Harrell, *Invisible Women: Junior Enlisted Army Wives*, Santa Monica, CA: RAND, 2000; M. C. Harrell, 'Army officers' spouses: have the white gloves been mothballed', *Armed Forces & Society* 28, 2001, pp. 55–75; W. Ruger, S. Wilson and S. Waddoups, 'Welfare and warfare: military service, combat and marital dissolution', *Armed Forces & Society* 29, 2002, pp. 86–107; R. Moelker and I. van der Kloet, 'Military families and the Armed Forces: a two-sided affair?', in G. Caforio (ed.), *Handbook of the Sociology of the Military*, New York: Kluwer, 2003; M. L. Kelley, 'The effects on deployment on traditional and nontraditional military families: Navy mothers and their children', in M. Ender (ed.), *Military Brats and Other Global Nomads: Growing Up in Organization Families*, Westport, MA: Praeger, 2002; M. Wertsch, *Military Brats: Legacies of Childhood Inside the Fortress*, New York: Harmony Books, 1991. For a critical feminist questioning of the relationship between military wives and the military, see C. Enloe, *Maneuvres: The International Politics of Militarizing Women's Lives*, Berkeley, CA: University of California Press, 2000, chapter 5.
2 For an introduction to the theories and methods of the discourse analytic approach and

methodology, see N. Fairclough, *Critical Discourse Analysis: The Critical Study of Language*, London: Longman, 1995; C. Weedon, *Feminist Practice and Poststructuralist Theory*, Oxford: Blackwell, 1987.

3 We should note, however, the growing recognition within the social science community of the value of a discourse analytic approach to the deconstruction of policy. See A. Hastings, 'Discourse and urban change: introduction to the special issue', *Urban Studies* 36, 1999, pp. 7–12; F. Fischer, *Reframing Public Policy: Discursive Politics and Deliberative Practices*, Oxford: Oxford University Press, 2003.

4 House of Commons debate on defence policy, 27 October 1997, Hansard Col 616.

5 Ministry of Defence, *Greater Opportunities for Women in the Army*, MoD press release 152/97, 27 October 1997.

6 George Robertson, speech at MoD Equal Opportunities conference 'Learning from Experience', Royal Society of Arts, London, 10 November 1998.

7 We make this point also in R. Woodward and P. Winter, 'Discourses of gender in the contemporary British Army', *Armed Forces & Society* 30, 2004, pp. 279–301.

8 MoD, *UK Armed Forces – Celebrating International Women's Day*, MoD press release 056/99, 8 March 1999. The UK MoD is not alone in doing this. A Canadian Department of National Defence press release for 5 March 2003 stated that 'As DND/CF personnel across the country prepare to celebrate International Women's Day the accomplishments of female soldiers, sailors, air personnel and civilian employees are being given the attention and recognition they deserve.'

9 C. Dandeker and F. Paton, *The Military and Social Change: A Personnel Strategy for the British Armed Forces*, London: Brassey's, 1997.

10 All figures calculated from Defence Analytic Services Agency data for the period April 1998 to April 2006.

11 C. Dandeker and M. W. Segal, 'Gender integration in Armed Forces: recent policy developments in the United Kingdom', *Armed Forces & Society* 23, 1996, pp. 29–46.

12 M. C. Harrell, M. K. Beckett and J. M. Sollinger, *The Status of Gender Integration in the Military: Analysis of Selected Occupations*, Santa Monica, CA: RAND, 2002.

13 N. J. Holden and L. M. Tanner, *An Examination of Current Gender Integration Policies and Practices in TTCP Nations*, Ottawa: The Technical Co-operation Programme Subcommittee on Non-atomic Military Research and Development, 2001.

14 Army Training and Recruiting Agency, personal communication to the authors, 11 August 1999.

15 Quoted in the *Daily Telegraph* 28 August 1997, 'Army unveils new training methods'.

16 This debate goes on and on; as we finish this book in the autumn of 2006, print media stories are emerging about the rising percentage of obese or overweight recruits, stories that themselves are part of a wider public debate about rising levels of obesity in the population in general and amongst children and teenagers in particular.

17 A. Beevor, 'The implications of social change on the British Army', *British Army Review* 104, 1993, pp. 14–22.

18 MoD, *Army training needs modernisation not mollycoddling, says Minister*, MoD press release 103/97, 27 August 1997.

19 I. M. M. Gemmell, 'Injuries among female army recruits: a conflict of legislation', *Ergonomics* 43, 2002, pp. 23–27.

20 J. L. J. Bilzon, *'Streaming' in British Army Recruit Training: Options for Change*, ATRA Report No: 2003.001, HQ ATRA, Upavon, 2003.

21 Adult Learning Inspectorate, *Safer Training: Managing Risks to the Welfare of Recruits in the British Armed Services*, Coventry: ALI, 2005, p. 40.

22 Bilzon, op. cit., p. 3.

23 ALI, op. cit., p. 15.

24 One of the first identifiable analyses of this was a CRE report on racism and discrimination in the Household Cavalry in 1996. The progress of equity issues around racism

and ethnicity are documented in C. Dandeker and D. Mason, 'The British Armed Services and the participation of minority ethnic communities: from equal opportunities to diversity?', *The Sociological Review* 49, 2001, 481–507; C. Dandeker and D. Mason, 'Diversifying the uniform: the participation of minority ethnic personnel in the British Armed Services', *Armed Forces &* Society 29, 2003, 481–508. Research into the experiences of different minority ethnic groups with regard to their British military participation is documented in A. Hussain, 'The British Armed Forces and the Hindu perspective', *Journal of Political and Military Sociology* 30 (1), 2002, 195–210; A. Hussain and M. Ishaq, 'British Pakistani Muslims' perceptions of the Armed Forces', *Armed Forces &* Society 28, 2002, 601–618; A. Hussain and M. Ishaq, 'Promoting equality of opportunity in the British Armed Forces: a "white" perspective', *Defence Studies* 3, 2003, 87–102.

25 The EOC was involved in a high-profile case brought by Angela Sirdar in 1999, a chef made redundant in 1995, whose offer of an employment transfer within the Royal Marines was withdrawn when it became apparent that she was a woman. The case was taken to the European Court of Justice, who ruled in the MoD's favour. The Royal Marines do not employ women. For a commentary by the EOC on the Sirdar case, see 'ECJ on exclusion of women from the Marines', *Equal Opportunities Review* 89, January/February 2000. For a wider commentary on the legal issues surrounding this and other cases in and beyond the UK, see G. Harries-Jenkins, 'Women in extended roles in the military: legal issues', *Current Sociology* 50, 2002, 745–769.

26 MoD, *Defence White Paper* Cm4446, London: The Stationery Office, 1999.

27 This directive has recently been superseded by Military Annual Training Test (MATT) 6 on Values and Standards.

28 ITD(A) 10, *Equal Opportunities* 2001.

29 Army, *Values and Standards of the British Army: A Guide for Soldiers*, 2002; Army, *Values and Standards: A Guide for Commanders*, 2002.

30 For an overview of these issues, see S. Liff and K. Dale, 'Formal opportunity, informal barriers: black women managers in a local authority', *Work, Employment and Society* 8, 1994, 177–198; S. Liff, 'Diversity and equal opportunities: room for constructive compromise', *Human Resource Management Journal* 9, 1999, 65–74; L. Dickens, 'Beyond the business case: a three-pronged approach to equality action', *Human Resource Management Journal* 9, 1999, 9–19.

31 MoD, *The Armed Forces Overarching Personnel Strategy*, London: MoD, 2000.

32 Army, *Guidance for the Employment of Women in the Army*, British Army Document D/DM (A)/76/04, 3 November 1997.

33 Army, *Equality and Diversity: Newsletter for Equal Opportunities Advisors*, Shrivenham: Tri-Service Equal Opportunities Training Centre, Winter 2002, p. 2.

34 Ibid.

35 MoD, 1999, op. cit., p.38.

36 Chief of the General Staff, *Equal Opportunities Directive for the Army, 2000*, British Army document, p. 4.

37 Army, 2002, op. cit., p. 1.

38 Ibid, p. 2.

39 Ibid, p. 1.

40 Interview with male army officer, 2002.

41 Army, *Values and Standards of the British Army: A Guide for Soldiers*, 2002. Army, *Values and Standards: A Guide for Commanders*, 2002. See also *Soldiering: The Military Covenant*, Army doctrine publication volume 5. These documents set out appropriate standards of social conduct, including avoiding social misbehaviour, drug misuse, alcohol abuse and irresponsible indebtedness; limits to contact with the media; and proscriptions on other unacceptable behaviour.

42 R. Woodward and T. Winter, 'Gender and the limits to diversity in the contemporary British Army', *Gender, Work and Organization* 13, 2006, pp. 45–67, p. 54.

43 S. L. Myers, 'Why diversity is a smokescreen for affirmative action', *Change*, 29 (July/August), 1997, pp. 24–32.
44 V. Basham, *An Analysis of Social Diversity in the British Armed Forces*, unpublished PhD thesis, Department of Politics, University of Bristol, 2006.
45 Interview with male Army officer, 2002.
46 ALI, op. cit., p. 5.
47 Ibid., p. 28.
48 Equal Opportunities Commission, *Equality in the 21st Century: A New Sex Equality Law for Britain*, London: EOC, 1999.
49 There is also evidence from the US that the potential of individual women to achieve promotion to senior positions is limited because of their exclusion from combat positions; see J. N. Baldwin, 'Female promotions in male-dominant organisations: the case of the US military', *The Journal of Politics* 58, 1996, pp. 1184–1197.
50 MoD, *Employment of women in the Armed Forces*, press release 126/02, 22 May 2002.
51 MoD, *The Wider Employment of Women in Ground Combat*, internal MoD briefing document.
52 Ibid.
53 J. Goldstein, *War and Gender: How Gender Shapes the War System and Vice Versa*, Cambridge: University of Cambridge Press, 2001, p. 199.
54 U. Ben-Shalom, Z. Lehre and E. Ben-Ari, 'Cohesion during military operations: a field study on combat units in the Al-Aqsa Intifada', *Armed Forces & Society* 32, 2005, pp. 63–79.
55 A. King, 'The word of command: communication and cohesion in the military', *Armed Forces & Society* 32, 2006, pp. 493–512.
56 This observation was borne out subsequently through the example of Captain Pip Tatershall who passed the all-arms Commando course in May 2002. This course has a very high attrition rate.
57 L. Rosen and L. Martin, 'Sexual harassment, cohesion and combat readiness in US Army support units', *Armed Forces & Society* 24, 1997, pp. 221–244.
58 The 1997 RAND study is cited in A. N. Wojach, 'Women can be integrated into ground combat units', in J. Haley (ed.), *Women in the Military*, San Diego, CA: Greenhaven, 2002, pp. 27–38.
59 Out gay men and lesbian women were officially barred from military service until 2000, but there is a literature suggesting that gay men and lesbian women have always served in the armed forces in Britain. See J. Heggie, *Uniform Identity: Lesbians and the Negotiation of Gender and Sexuality in the British Army since 1950*, unpublished PhD thesis, University of York, 2005; E. Hall, *We Can't Even March Straight*, London: Vintage, 1995; P. Higgins, *Heterosexual Dictatorship: Male Homosexuality in Postwar Britain*, London: Fourth Estate, 1996, chapter 2. For a queer, critical and anti-militarist discussion, see P. Tatchell, *We Don't Want to March Straight*, London: Cassell, 1995. For a discussion of sexuality and military participation in the Israeli context, see D. Kaplan and E. Ben-Ari, 'Brothers and others in arms: managing gay identity in combat units of the Israeli Army', *Journal of Contemporary Ethnography* 29, 2000, pp. 396–432; A. Belkin and M. Levitt, 'Homosexuality and the Israeli Defense Forces: did lifting the gay ban undermine military performance?', *Armed Forces and Society* 27, 2001, pp. 541–565. For histories of the experience in the US armed forces, see L. Murphy, *Perverts by Official Order: The Campaign Against Homosexuals in the United States Navy*, New York: Harrington Park Press, 1988; R. Shilts, *Conduct Unbecoming: Gays and Lesbians in the US Military*, New York: St. Martin's Press, 1993; G. L. Lehring, *Officially Gay: The Political Construction of Sexuality by the US Military*, Philadelphia, PA: Temple University Press, 2003.
60 ALI, op. cit.
61 Ibid, pp. 43–44

62 House of Commons Defence Committee, *Duty of Care*, Third Report of Session 2004-05, HC63-1, London: The Stationery Office, 2005.
63 S. Rutherford, R. Schneider and A. Walmsley, *Ministry of Defence/Equal Opportunities Commission Agreement on Preventing and Dealing Effectively with Sexual Harassment: Quantitative and Qualitative Research into Sexual Harassment in the Armed Forces*, London: Schneider Ross, 2006.
64 See the *Equality and Diversity Action Plan for the Army, 2006–07*, with its strategies for the elimination of racist, sexist, homophobic and other unacceptable behaviour.
65 Rutherford *et al.*, op. cit., p. 9.
66 ALI, op. cit., p. 28.
67 D. M. Dean, *Warriors Without Weapons: The Victimization of Military Women.* Pasadena, TX: Minerva Centre, 1997.
68 L. Miller, 'Not just weapons of the weak: gender harassment as a form of protest for Army men', *Social Psychology Quarterly* 60, 1997, pp. 32–51.
69 J. M. Firestone and R. J. Harris, 'Perceptions of effectiveness of responses to sexual harassment in the US Military, 1988 and 1995', *Gender Work and Organization* 10, 2003, pp. 42–64.
70 M. Herbert, *Camouflage Isn't Only for Combat: Gender, Sexuality and Women in the Military*, New York: New York University Press, 1998, p. 112.

4 Masculinities and the British Army

1 K. Lukowiak, *Marijuana Time: Join the Army, See the World, Meet Interesting People and Smoke All Their Dope*, London: Orion, 2000, p. 9.
2 P. Higate (ed.), *Military Masculinities: Identity and the State*, Westport, CT: Praeger, 2003; P. R. Higate, 'Theorizing continuity: from military to civilian life', *Armed Forces & Society*, 27 (3), 2001, pp. 443–460; P. Higate, 'The body resists: everyday clerking and unmilitary practice', in S. Nettleton and J. Watson (eds), *The Body in Everyday Life*, London: Routledge, 1998; P. Higate, 'Soldiering on? Theorising homelessness amongst ex-servicemen', in R. Burrows, N. Place and D. Quilgars (eds), *Homelessness and Social Policy*, London: Routledge, 1997; P. Higate, 'Tough bodies and rough sleeping: embodying homelessness amongst ex-servicemen', *Housing, Theory and Society*, 17, 2000, pp. 97–108; B. Connell, 'Masculinity, violence and war', in M. Kimmel and M. Messner (eds), *Men's Lives*, 3rd edn, Boston, MA: Allyn and Bacon, 1995; R. W. Connell, *Masculinities*, Cambridge: Polity Press, 1995; R. W. Connell, *The Men and the Boys*, London: Polity, 2000; D. H. J. Morgan, 'Theater of war: combat, the military, and masculinities', in H. Brod and M. Kaufman (eds), *Theorising Masculinities*, London: Sage, 1994; R. Woodward, 'Warrior heroes and little green men: soldiers, military training, and the construction of rural masculinities', *Rural Sociology*, 64 (4), 2000, pp. 640–657; R. Woodward, 'It's a Man's Life! Soldiers, masculinity and the countryside', *Gender, Place and Culture*, 5 (3), 1998, pp. 277–300; L. H. Bowker (ed.), *Masculinities and Violence*, Beverly Hills, CA: Sage, 1998.
3 Ibid. p. 165.
4 J. Hopton, 'The state and military masculinity', in Higate, op. cit; Connell, op. cit.
5 S. Nixon, *Hard Looks: Masculinities, Spectatorship and Contemporary Consumption*, London: UCL Press, 1996.
6 Higate, 2003, op. cit.
7 Connell, 2000, op. cit.
8 J. Weeks, *Sexuality and its Discontents*, London: Routledge, 1985; S. Nixon, op. cit.
9 http://shared.armyjobs.mod.uk/JobDescriptions/RegularArmy/Combat/Infantry/InfantrySoldier.htm, accessed 9 December 2006.
10 See Brown, for an analysis of constructions of masculinity in post Cold War British Army recruitment literature: http://www.ssrc.org/programs/gsc/gsc_quarterly/newsletter5/content/brown.page, accessed 9 December 2006.

11 S. Nixon, 'Exhibiting masculinity', in S. Hall (ed.), *Representation: Cultural Representations and Signifying Practices*, London: Sage, 1997.
12 Higate, op. cit., p. 130.
13 B. Connell, op. cit.
14 J. Butler, *Gender Trouble: Feminism and the Subversion of Identity*, New York: Routledge, 1990, p. 140.
15 http://www.armyjobs.mod.uk/RegularArmy/RolesAndCareers/, accessed 9 December 2006.
16 See http://www.armyjobs.mod.uk/RegularArmy/RolesAndCareers/, accessed 9 December 2006.
17 http://shared.armyjobs.mod.uk/JobDescriptions/RegularArmy/Specialist/Musician.htm, accessed 9 December 2006.
18 http://www.army.mod.uk/atr/atr_winchester/training/index.htm, accessed 9 December 2006.
19 http://www.army.mod.uk/atr/atr_winchester/training/index.htm, accessed 9 December 2006.
20 http://www.armyjobs.mod.uk, accessed 9 December 2006.
21 Connell, op. cit; Morgan, op. cit; Hockey, op. cit.
22 See Paul Higate's work on masculinities and peace-keeping in sub-Saharan Africa: P. Higate, 'Men, masculinities and peacekeeping: training for peace in sub-Saharan Africa', working paper for the Norwegian Institute for International Affairs (NUPI), Oslo, 2004.
23 Hockey, op. cit.; J. Hockey, *Squaddies: Portrait of a Subculture*, Exeter: University of Exeter, 1986; J. Hockey, ' "Head down, Bergen on, mind in neutral": the infantry body', *Journal of Political and Military Sociology*, 30 (1), 2002, 148–171.
24 R. Woodward, ' "Not for Queen and country or any of that shit . . .": reflections on citizenship and military participation in contemporary British soldier narratives', in E. Gilbert and D. Cowan (eds), *War, Citizenship, Territory*, London: Routledge, 2007.
25 For an introduction to these debates, see N. King, *Memory, Narrative, Identity: Remembering the Self*, Edinburgh: Edinburgh University Press, 2000; L. Anderson, *Autobiography*, New York: Routledge, 2001.
26 S. Hynes, *The Soldier's Tale: Bearing Witness to Modern War*, London: Pimlico, 1997.
27 For a good overview of these issues, see A. Vernon (ed.), *Arms and the Self: War, the Military and Autobiographical Writing*, Kent, OH: Kent State University Press, 2005.
28 Y. N. Harari, 'Martial illusions: war and disillusionment in twentieth-century and Renaissance military memoirs', *Journal of Military History*, 69, 2005, p. 71.
29 Morgan, op. cit; R. Woodward, 'Locating military masculinities: space, place, and the formation of gender identity and the British Army', in Higate, op. cit; J. Hockey, ' "Head down, Bergen on, mind in neutral" '; M. Foucault, *Discipline and Punish: The Birth of the Prison*, London: Penguin, 1977.
30 A. van Gennep, *The Rites of Passage*, London: Routledge and Kegan Paul, 1960 [1909].
31 D. Morgan, 'It will make a man of you: notes on National Service, masculinity and autobiography,' *Studies in Sexual Politics*, 1987, pp. 1–90.
32 Hockey, op. cit., p. 16.
33 Morgan, 1994, op. cit.
34 V. Woolf, 1992, p. 120 in S. Andermahr, T. Lovell and C. Wolkowitz, *A Concise Glossary of Feminist Theory*, London: Arnold, 1997.
35 Hockey, 2003, op. cit.
36 van Gennep, op. cit.
37 Hockey, 2003, op. cit., p. 16.
38 Hockey, 2003, op. cit., p. 17.
39 A. Ballinger, *The Quiet Soldier: On Selection with 21 SAS*, London: Orion, 1992.

40 J. Bourke, *Dismembering the Male: Men's Bodies, Britain and the Great War*, London: Reaktion Books, 1996.
41 Personal communication, December 2006.
42 Hockey, 2002, op. cit., p. 150.
43 W. H. McNeill, *Keeping Together in Time: Dance and Drill in Human History*, Cambridge, MA: Harvard University Press, 1995; Hockey, 2002, op. cit., p. 151.
44 Bourke, op. cit., pp. 130–131.
45 Ibid.
46 Preece, 2004, p. 246.
47 http://www.youtube.com/watch?v=jjhxekdZl7k, accessed 9 December 2006.
48 In the original video, which took the its music to the number one chart position, Kay mimes to the jaunty Tony Christie song 'Is this the way to Amarillo', while marching along a series of corridors, roads and paths and is joined on his journey by a series of celebrities.
49 http://news.bbc.co.uk/1/hi/uk/4554083.stm, accessed 9 December 2006.
50 Preece, op. cit., p.51
51 McNab, 1993, p. 13.
52 Ibid.
53 Ibid. p. 59.
54 Lukowiak, op. cit., p.101
55 Hockey, 2003, op. cit., p. 22
56 Preece, p. 244.
57 Preece, p. 257.
58 Bramley, 2006, p. 272.
59 M. Bakhtin, *Rabelais and His World*, Bloomington, IL: Indiana University Press, 1984. For a concise introduction to the notion of the carnivalesque, see J. Storey, *An Introduction to Cultural Theory and Popular Culture*, 2nd edn, Hemel Hempstead: Harvester Wheatsheaf, 1993.
60 J. Storey, op. cit.
61 Hockey, 2003, op. cit., p. 22.
62 Morgan, D., 1994, op. cit., p. 167.
63 Hockey, op. cit., p. 23.
64 http://www.shinycapstar.com/pacesticking05.htm, accessed 9 December 2006.
65 Butler, J. (1990) *Gender Trouble: Feminism and the Subversion of Identity*, New York: Routledge.
66 Lukowiak, op. cit., p. 49.
67 Lukowiak op. cit., p. 88.
68 Ibid.
69 The Soldier's Creed explains itself as follows: 'In line with the British Army's Values and Standards, this short video has been created to emphasise what it means to be a British Army soldier. It is our creed. We shall fight by it for our country.' This little genre of home-made patriotic videos features iconography like Union Jacks, the national anthem and silhouetted (therefore abstracted, essentialised) images of soldiers.
70 ESRC funded project 'Negotiating Identity and Representation in the Mediated Armed Forces': Rachel Woodward, Trish Winter and K. Neil Jenkings, Newcastle University, 2006–7.
71 Morgan, D., 1994, op. cit., p. 166.
72 Higate, 2004, op. cit.
73 Higate, 2004, op. cit., and Higate 2003, op. cit.
74 F. Barrett, 'Gender strategies of women professionals: the case of the US Navy', in M. Dent and S. Whitehead (eds), *Managing Professional Identities: Knowledge, Performativity and the 'New' Professional*, London: Routledge, p. 64. See also Agostino.

75 Barrett, op. cit., p. 169.
76 O. Sasson-Levy, 'Feminism and military gender practices: Israeli women soldiers in "masculine" roles', *Sociological Inquiry*, 73 (3), 2003, p. 447.
77 Y. Tasker, 'Soldiers' stories: women and military masculinities in *Courage Under Fire*', *Quarterly Review of Film & Video*, 19, 2002, pp. 209–222.
78 Halberstam, cited in Tasker, op. cit.
79 Sasson-Levy, op. cit.
80 S. Ford, *One Up: A Woman in Action with the SAS*, London: Harper Collins, 1997, p. 141.
81 Sasson-Levy, op. cit., p. 459.

5 Gender and the soldier in the British media and popular culture

1 M. Macdonald, *Exploring Media Discourse*, London: Arnold, 2003.
2 Ibid. p. 20.
3 Ibid. p. 21.
4 Ibid. p. 21.
5 M. Foucault, 1990, 1976, *The History of Sexuality. Volume 1: An Introduction*, London: Penguin, p. 105.
6 K. Woodward, 'Motherhood: identities, meanings and myths', in K. Woodward (ed.), *Identity and Difference*, London: Sage, 1997, p. 255.
7 For example, McNab, 1998.
8 Ryan, 1995; Spence, 1998; Stancovic, 2001; McManners, 2002; Swofford, 2003.
9 F. Bonami, M. L. Frisa *et al. Uniform*, Milano: Charter, 2000.
10 http://www.imdb.com/title/tt0106138/usercomments, accessed 16 October 2006.
11 B. Carson and Lewellyn-Jones (eds), *Frames and Fictions on Television*, Exeter: Intellect, 2000.
12 J. Jacobs, *Body Trauma TV: The New Hospital Dramas*, London: British Film Institute, 2003.
13 *The Sun*, 6 April 2001.
14 See, for example, *News of the World*, 11 February 2001.
15 *The Sun*, 6 April 2001.
16 http://www.thesun.co.uk/article/0,,2-2005570450,00.html, accessed 30 June 2006.
17 *The Daily Telegraph*, 3 April 2001.
18 *The Sun*, 26 April 2001.
19 Accessed 31 May 2002.
20 R. Dyer, *Stars*, London: British Film Institute, 1979.
21 http://www.imdb.com/title/tt0106138/, accessed 17 October 2006.
22 DVD, *Series 3 Ultimate Force* (2005), Bentley Productions for the ITV Network.
23 For an example of audience reaction to the changes in the show, see, for example, http://en.wikipedia.org/wiki/Ultimate_Force, accessed 27 October 2006.

6 The politicis of gender and the contemporary British Army

1 Stuart Hall argues this about national identity: S. Hall (ed.), *Representation: Cultural Representations and Signifying Practices*, London: Sage, p. 236.
2 See, for example, D. Campbell, *Writing Security: United States Foreign Policy and the Politics of Identity*, Manchester: Manchester University Press, 1998; S. Dalby, *Creating the Second Cold War: The Discourse of Politics*, London: Pinter, 1990; S. Dalby, *Environmental Security*, Minneapolis, MN: University of Minnesota Press, 2002; G. Ó Tuathail, *Critical Geopolitics: The Politics of Writing Global Space*, London: Routledge, 1997; G. Ó Tuathail and S. Dalby (eds), *Rethinking Geopolitics*, London: Routledge, 1998.
3 K. Davis and V. Thomas, *Chief Land Staff Gender Integration Study: The Experience*

of Women Who Have Served in the Combat Arts, Personnel Research Team, Sponsor Research Report 98-1, Department of National Defence, Canada: Ottawa, 1998. Quoted in D. Winslow and J. Dunn, 'Women in the Canadian Forces: between legal and social integration', *Current Sociology* 50, 2002, 641–667.

4 Ibid, p. 662.

5 F. Barrett, 'Gender strategies of women professionals', in M. Dent and S. Whitehead (eds), *Managing Professional Identities: Knowledge, Performativity and the 'New' Professional*, London: Routledge, 2002, pp. 157–173.

6 K. Agostino, ' "She's a good hand": Navy women's strategies in masculinist workplaces', *Journal of Interdisciplinary Gender Studies* 3, 1998, pp. 1–22.

7 Leah Mates, awarded damages for sexual harassment, quoted from BBC News, website, 'Female spy makes harassment claim', www.bbc.co.uk, accessed 8 November 2005.

8 MoD and Equal Opportunities Commission, *Agreement between the Ministry of Defence and the Equal Opportunities Commission on Preventing and Dealing Effectively with Sexual Harassment in the Armed Forces: Progress Report and Phase Three Action Plan, 2006*, Measure 15, Gender Balance in Training.

9 Ibid.

10 Staff Sergeant A. T. R. Pirbright, *Soldiers to Be*, series 1, episode 1, 'A New Life', broadcast on BBC Television, 3 August 1999, quoted in R. Woodward, 'Locating military masculinities', in P. Higate (ed.), *Military Masculinities: Identity and the State*, Greenwood, IN: Westport, 2003, p. 48.

11 Anthony Forster warns of the dangers around the breakdown in the military covenant between military personnel and their political and military leadership; see A. Forster, 'Breaking the covenant: governance of the British Army in the 21st century', *International Affairs* 82, 2006, pp. 1101–1115.

Bibliography

Adie, K. *Corsets to Camouflage: Women and War*, London: Hodder & Stoughton, 2003.

Adult Learning Inspectorate, *Safer Training: Managing Risks to the Welfare of Recruits in the British Armed Services*, Coventry: Adult Learning Inspectorate, 2005.

Agostino, K. 'Masculinity, sexuality and life on board Her Majesty's Royal Australian ships', *Journal of Interdisciplinary Gender Studies* 2 (1), 1997, pp. 15–30.

—— ' "She's a good hand": Navy women's strategies in masculinist workplaces', *Journal of Interdisciplinary Gender Studies* 3 (1), 1998, pp. 1–22.

—— 'Women in uniform: challenging feminisms', in K. Spurling and E. Greenhalgh (eds), *Women in Uniform: Perceptions and Pathways*, Canberra: ADFA, 2000, pp. 64–82

Alt, B. S. and B. S. Stone, *Campfollowing: A History of the Military Wife*, Praeger, New York, 1991.

Anderson, L. *Autobiography*, New York: Routledge, 2001.

Army, *Guidance for the Employment of Women in the Army.* British Army Document D/DM (A)/76/04, 3 November 1997.

—— *Equality and Diversity: Newsletter for Equal Opportunities Advisors*, Shrivenham: Tri-Service Equal Opportunities Training Centre, Winter 2002.

—— *Values and Standards: A Guide for Commanders*, 2002.

—— *Values and Standards of the British Army: A Guide for Soldiers*, 2002.

Bakhtin, M. *Rabelais and His World*, Bloomington, IN: Indiana University Press, 1984.

Baldwin, J. N. 'Female promotions in male-dominant organisations: the case of the US military', *Journal of Politics* 58, 1996, pp. 1184–1197.

Ballinger, A. *The Quiet Soldier: On Selection with 21 SAS*, London: Orion, 1992.

Barrett, F. 'Gender strategies of women professionals: the case of the US Navy', in M. Dent and S. Whitehead (eds), *Managing Professional Identities: Knowledge, Performativity and the 'New' Professional*, London: Routledge, 2002.

—— 'Gender strategies of women professionals', in M. Dent and S. Whitehead (eds), *Managing Professional Identities: Knowledge, Performativity and the 'New' Professional*, London: Routledge, 2002.

Basham, V. (2006) *An Analysis of Social Diversity in the British Armed Forces*, unpublished PhD thesis, Department of Politics, University of Bristol.

Beevor, A. 'The implications of social change on the British Army', *British Army Review* 104, 1993, pp. 14–22.

Belkin, A. and A. Levitt, 'Homosexuality and the Israeli Defense Forces: did lifting the gay ban undermine military performance?', *Armed Forces and Society* 27, 2001, pp. 541–565.

Ben-Shalom, U., Z. Lehre and E. Ben-Ari, 'Cohesion during military operations: a field study on combat units in the Al-Aqsa Intifada', *Armed Forces & Society* 32, 2005, pp. 63–79.

Bidwell, S. *The Women's Royal Army Corps*, London: Leo Cooper, 1977.

Bilzon, J. L. J. *'Streaming' in British Army Recruit Training: Options for Change.* ATRA Report No: 2003.001, HQ ATRA, Upavon, 2003.

Bonami, F., M. L. Frisa and S. Tronchi, *Uniform*, Milan: Charter, 2000

Boulègue, J. '"Feminization" and the French military: an anthropological approach', *Armed Forces & Society* 17 (3), 1991, pp. 343–363.

Bourke, J. *Dismembering the Male: Men's Bodies, Britain and the Great War*, London: Reaktion Books, 1996.

Bowker, L. H. (ed.) *Masculinities and Violence*, Beverly Hills, CA: Sage, 1998.

Bracken, P. 'Women in the Army', in H. Strachan (ed.), *The British Army: Manpower and Society into the Twenty-First Century*, London: Frank Cass, 2000.

Braybon, G. and P. Summerfield, *Out of the Cage: Women's Experiences in Two World Wars*, London: Pandora, 1987.

Butler, J. *Gender Trouble: Feminism and the Subversion of Identity*, New York: Routledge, 1990.

—— *Bodies That Matter: On the Discursive Limits of 'Sex'*, London: Routledge, 1994.

Campbell, D. *Writing Security: United States Foreign Policy and the Politics of Identity*, Manchester: Manchester University Press, 1998.

Carreiras, H. 'Women in the Portuguese Armed Forces: from visibility to "eclipse" ', *Current Sociology* 50 (5), 2002, pp. 678–714.

Carson, B. and M. Lewellyn-Jones (eds) *Frames and Fictions on Television*, Exeter: Intellect, 2000.

Chandler, D. and I. Beckett, *The Oxford History of the British Army*, Oxford: Oxford University Press, 1996.

—— and R. Holmes (ed.) *The Oxford Companion to Military History*, Oxford: Oxford University Press, 2001.

Chief of the General Staff, *Equal Opportunities Directive for the Army, 2000*. British Army Document, 2000.

Committee on Women in the NATO Forces (2006) *France.* National Briefings and reports. Available at: http://www.nato.int/ims/2006/win/pdf/france_national_report%202006.pdf, accessed 30 October 2006.

—— *United States.* National Briefings and reports. Available at: http://www.nato.int/ims/2006/win/pdf/us_brief.pdf, accessed 11 November 2006.

Connell, R. W. 'Masculinity, violence and war', in P. Patton and R. Poole (eds), *War/Masculinity*, Sydney: Intervention, 1985.

—— *Masculinities*, Cambridge: Polity Press, 1995.

—— 'Masculinity, violence and war', in M. Kimmel and M. Messner (eds), *Men's Lives*, 3rd edn, Boston, MA: Allyn & Bacon, 1995.

—— *The Men and the Boys*, London: Polity Press, 2000.

van Creveld, M. 'Less than we can be: men, women and the modern military', *Journal of Strategic Studies* 23 (4), 2000, pp. 1–20.

—— *Men, Women and War*, London: Cassell, 2001.

Crim, B. 'Silent partners: women and warfare in Early Modern Europe', in G. J. DeGroot and C. Peniston-Bird (eds), *A Soldier and a Woman: Sexual Integration in the Military*, Harlow: Longman, 2000, pp. 18–32.

Dalby, S. *Creating the Second Cold War: The Discourse of Politics*, London: Pinter, 1990.

—— *Environmental Security*, Minneapolis, MN: University of Minnesota Press, 2002.

Dandeker, C. 'Armed Forces and society research in the United Kingdom: a review of British military sociology', in G. Kümmel and A. G. Prüfert (eds), *Military Sociology: The Richness of a Discipline*, Baden-Baden: Nomos, 2000, pp. 68–90.

—— and D. Mason, 'The British Armed Services and the participation of minority ethnic communities: From equal opportunities to diversity?', *The Sociological Review* 49, 2001, pp. 481–507.

—— and D. Mason, 'Diversifying the uniform: the participation of minority ethnic personnel in the British Armed Services', *Armed Forces &* Society 29, 2003, pp. 481–508.

—— and F. Paton, *The Military and Social Change: A Personnel Strategy for the British Armed Forces*, London: Brassey's, 1997.

—— and M. W. Segal, 'Gender integration in the Armed Forces: recent policy developments in the United Kingdom', *Armed Forces & Society* 23 (1), 1996, pp. 29–47.

—— and A. Strachan, 'Soldier recruitment in the British Army: a spatial and social methodology for analysis and monitoring', *Armed Forces & Society* 19 (2), 1993, pp. 279–290.

Dar, Y. and S. Kimhi, 'Youth in the military: gendered experiences in the conscript service in the Israeli Army', *Armed Forces & Society* 30 (3), 2004, pp. 433–459.

Davis K. and V. Thomas, *Chief Land Staff Gender Integration Study: The Experience of Women Who Have Served in the Combat Arts*, Personnel Research Team, Sponsor Research Report 98-1, Department of National Defence, Ottawa, Canada, 1998.

Dawson, G. *Soldier Heroes: British Adventure, Empire and the Imagining of Masculinity*, London: Routledge, 1994.

Dean, D. M. *Warriors Without Weapons: The Victimization of Military Women*, Pasadena, CA: Minerva Centre, 1997.

Degroot, G. J. 'A few good women: gender stereotypes, the military and peacekeeping', *International Peacekeeping* 8 (2), 2001, pp. 23–38.

Department of Defence, *Women in the Australian Defence Force*. Australian Government website: www.defence.gov.au/equity/women.htm, accessed 28 February 2005.

Dickens, L. 'Beyond the business case: a three-pronged approach to equality action', *Human Resource Management Journal* 9, 1999, pp. 9–19.

Dyer, R. *Stars*, London: British Film Institute, 1979.

Enloe, C. *Maneuvres: The International Politics of Militarizing Women's Lives*, Berkeley, CA: University of California Press, 2000.

Equal Opportunities Commission, *Equality in the 21st Century: A New Sex Equality Law for Britain*, London: EOC, 1999.

Fairclough, N. *Critical Discourse Analysis: The Critical Study of Language*, London: Longman, 1995.

Feinman, I. R. *Citizenship Rites: Feminist Soldiers and Feminist Antimilitarists*, New York: New York University Press, 2000.

Firestone, J. M. and R. J. Harris, 'Perceptions of effectiveness of responses to sexual harassment in the US Military, 1988 and 1995', *Gender Work and Organization* 10, 2003, pp. 42–64.

Fischer, F. *Reframing Public Policy: Discursive Politics and Deliberative Practices*, Oxford: Oxford University Press, 2003.

Ford, S. *One Up: A Woman in Action with the SAS*, London: Harper Collins, 1997, p. 141.

Forster, A. *Armed Forces and Society in Europe*, London: Palgrave Macmillan, 2005.

—— 'Breaking the covenant: governance of the British Army in the 21st century', *International Affairs* 82, 2006, pp. 1101–1115.

Foster, K. *Fighting Fictions: War, Narrative and National Identity*, London: Pluto Press, 1999.

Foucault, M. *Discipline and Punish: The Birth of the Prison*, London: Penguin, 1977.

——*The History of Sexuality. Volume 1: An Introduction*, London: Penguin, 1990 [1976] p. 105.

Fowler, C. 'Integration of women into the Armed Services of the UK', in K. Spurling and E. Greenhalgh (eds), *Women in Uniform: Perceptions and Pathways*, Canberra: UNSW at ADFA, 2000, pp. 141–151.

French, D. *Military Identities: The Regimental System, the British Army and the British People, 1870–2000*, Oxford: Oxford University Press, 2006.

Frost, G. 'How to destroy an Army', in G. Frost (ed.), *Not Fit to Fight: The Cultural Subversion of the Armed Forces in Britain and America*, London: Social Affairs Unit, 1998.

—— (ed.) *Not Fit to Fight: The Cultural Subversion of the Armed Forces in Britain and America*, London: Social Affairs Unit, 1998.

Gat, A. 'Female participation in war: biocultural interactions', *Journal of Strategic Studies* 23 (4), 2000, pp. 21–31.

Gatens, M. *Imaginary Bodies: Ethics, Power and Corporeality*, London: Indiana University Press, 1996.

Gemmell, I. M. M. 'Injuries among female army recruits: a conflict of legislation', *Ergonomics* 43, 2002, pp. 23–27.

van Gennep, A. *The Rites of Passage*, London: Routledge and Kegan Paul, 1960 [1909].

Giddens, A. *The Nation-State and Violence*, Berkeley, CA: University of California Press, 1987.

Gillies, M. *Waiting for Hitler: Voices from Britain on the Brink of Invasion*, London: Hodder & Stoughton, 2006.

Goldstein, J. *War and Gender: How Gender Shapes the War System and Vice Versa*, Cambridge: Cambridge University Press, 2001.

Gullace, N. *The Blood of Our Sons: Men, Women and the Renegotiation of British Citizenship during the First World War*, London: Palgrave Macmillan, 2002.

Gutmann, S. *The Kinder, Gentler Military: Can America's Gender-Neutral Fighting Force Still Win Wars?* New York: Scribner, 2000.

Hagemann, K. and S. Schüler-Springorum (eds) *Home/Front: The Military, War and Gender in Twentieth Century Germany*, Oxford: Berg, 2000.

Hall, E. *We Can't Even March Straight*, London: Vintage, 1995.

Hall, S. (ed.) *Representation: Cultural Representations and Signifying Practices*, London: Sage (in association with The Open University), 1997.

Harari, Y. N. 'Martial illusions: war and disillusionment in twentieth-century and Renaissance military memoirs', *Journal of Military History* 69, 2005, p. 71.

Harrell, M. C. *Invisible Women: Junior Enlisted Army Wives*, Santa Monica, CA: RAND, 2000.

—— 'Army officers' spouses: have the white gloves been mothballed', *Armed Forces & Society* 28, 2001, pp. 55–75.

——, M. K. Beckett and J. M. Sollinger, *The Status of Gender Integration in the Military: Analysis of Selected Occupations*, Santa Monica, CA: RAND, 2002.

Harries-Jenkins, G. 'Women in extended roles in the Military: legal issues', *Current Sociology* 50, 2002, pp. 745–769.

Harris, M. 'Recognizing the role of women in NATO's military forces', *NATO Review* 45 (5), 1997, pp. 25–26.

Hastings, A. 'Discourse and urban change: introduction to the special issue', *Urban Studies* 36, 1999, 7–12.

Heggie, J. *Uniform Identity: Lesbians and the Negotiation of Gender and Sexuality in the British Army since 1950*, unpublished PhD thesis, University of York, 2005.

Heinecken, L. 'Affirming gender equality: the challenges facing the South African armed forces', *Current Sociology* 50 (5), 2002, pp. 715–728.

Hendrix, S. N. 'In the Army: women, camp followers and gender roles in the British Army in the French and Indian Wars, 1755–1765', in G. J. DeGroot and C. Peniston-Bird (eds), *A Soldier and a Woman: Sexual Integration in the Military*, Harlow: Longman, 2000, pp. 33–48.

Herbert, M. *Camouflage Isn't Only for Combat: Gender, Sexuality and Women in the Military*, New York: New York University Press, 1998.

Hickman, T. *The Call-Up: A History of National Service*, London: Headline, 2004.

Higate, P. R. 'Soldiering on? Theorising homelessness amongst ex-servicemen', in R. Burrows, N. Place and D. Quilgars (eds), *Homelessness and Social Policy*, London: Routledge, 1997.

—— 'The body resists: everyday clerking and unmilitary practice', in S. Nettleton and J. Watson (eds), *The Body in Everyday Life*, London: Routledge, 1998.

—— 'Tough bodies and rough sleeping: embodying homelessness amongst ex-servicemen', *Housing, Theory and Society*, 17, 2000, pp. 97–108.

—— 'Theorizing continuity: from military to civilian life', *Armed Forces & Society*, 27 (3), Spring 2001, pp. 443–460.

—— (ed.) *Military Masculinities: Identity and the State*, Westport, CT: Praeger, 2003.

—— ' "Soft clerks" and "hard civvies": pluralizing military masculinities', in P. R. Higate (ed.), *Military Masculinities: Identity and the State*, Westport, CT: Praeger, 2003.

—— 'Men, masculinities and peacekeeping: training for peace in sub-Saharan Africa', working paper for the Norwegian Institute for International Affairs (NUPI) Oslo, 2004.

Higate, P. R. and A. Cameron, *Heterosexual Dictatorship: Male Homosexuality in Postwar Britain*, London: Fourth Estate, 1996.

—— 'Reflexivity and researching the military', *Armed Forces & Society* 32 (2), 2006, pp. 219–233.

Higonnet, M. *Nurses at the Front: Writing the Wounds of the Great War*, New Haven, CT: Northeastern University Press, 2001.

——, J. Jenson, S. Michel and M. C. Weitz (eds), *Behind the Lines: Gender and the Two World Wars*, Whitehaven, MD: Yale University Press, 1987.

Hockey, J. ' "Head down, Bergen on, mind in neutral": the infantry body', *Journal of Political and Military Sociology*, 2002, 30 (1), pp. 148–171.

Hockey, J. *Squaddies: Portrait of a Subculture*, Exeter: University of Exeter, 1986.

Holden N. J. and L. M. Tanner, *An Examination of Current Gender Integration Policies and Practices in TTCP Nations*, Ottawa: The Technical Co-operation Programme Subcommittee on Non-Atomic Military Research and Development, 2001.

Hong, D.-S. 'Women in the South Korean Military', *Current Sociology* 50 (5), 2002, pp. 729–743.

Hopton, J. 'The State and military masculinity', in P. Higate (ed.), *Military Masculinities: Identity and the State*, Westport, CT: Prager, 2003.

House of Commons Defence Committee, *Duty of Care*. Third Report of Session 2004–05, HC63-1, London: The Stationery Office, 2005.

Hussain, A. 'The British Armed Forces and the Hindu perspective', *Journal of Political and Military Sociology* 30 (1), 2002, pp. 195–210.

—— and M. Ishaq, 'British Pakistani Muslims' perceptions of the Armed Forces', *Armed Forces & Society* 28, 2002, pp. 601–618.

—— and M. Ishaq, 'Promoting equality of opportunity in the British Armed Forces: a "white" perspective', *Defence Studies* 3, 2003, pp. 87–102.

Hynes, S. *The Soldier's Tale: Bearing Witness to Modern War*, London: Pimlico, 1997.

Iskra, D., S. Trainor, M. Leithauser and M. W. Segal, 'Women's participation in armed forces cross-nationally: expanding Segal's model', *Current Sociology* 50 (5), 2002, pp. 771–797.

Jabri, V. 'War, security and the liberal state', *Security Dialogue* 37 (1), 2006, pp. 47–64.

Jacobs, J. *Body Trauma TV: The New Hospital Dramas*, London: British Film Institute, 2003.

Jacobs, S., R. Jacobson and J. Marchbank (eds) *States of Conflict: Gender, Violence and Resistance*, London: Zed Books, 2000.

Johnson, S. S. *All Bull: The National Servicemen*, London: Allison and Busby, 1973.

Kaplan, D. and E. Ben-Ari, 'Brothers and others in arms: managing gay identity in combat units of the Israeli Army', *Journal of Contemporary Ethnography* 29, 2000, pp. 396–432.

Kelley, M. L. 'The effects on deployment on traditional and nontraditional military families: Navy mothers and their children', in M. Ender (ed.), *Military Brats and Other Global Nomads: Growing Up in Organization Families*, Westport, CT: Praeger, 2002.

King, A. 'The word of command: communication and cohesion in the military', *Armed Forces & Society* 32, 2006, pp. 493–512.

King, N. *Memory, Narrative, Identity: Remembering the Self*, Edinburgh: Edinburgh University Press, 2000.

Kipling, R. *The Complete Barrack Room Ballads of Rudyard Kipling*, C. Carrington (ed.), London: Methuen, 1973.

Klein, U. ' "Our best boys": the gendered nature of civil–military relations in Israel', *Men and Masculinities* 2 (1), 1999, pp. 47–65.

—— 'The gender perspective of civil–military relations in Israeli society', *Current Sociology* 50 (5), 2002, pp. 669–686.

Kümmel, G. 'When boy meets girl: the "feminization" of the military: an introduction also to be read as a post-script', *Current Sociology* 50 (5), 2002, pp. 615–639.

—— 'Complete access: women in the Bundeswehr and male ambivalence', *Armed Forces & Society* 28 (4), 2002, pp. 555–573.

Laliberte, L. and D. Harrison, *No Life Like It: Military Wives in Canada*, Toronto: J. Lorimer, 1994.

Lehring, G. L. *Officially Gay: The Political Construction of Sexuality by the US Military*, Philadelphia, PA: Temple University Press, 2003.

Liff, S. 'Diversity and equal opportunities: room for constructive compromise', *Human Resource Management Journal* 9, 1999, pp. 65–74.

—— and K. Dale, 'Formal opportunity, informal barriers: black women managers in a local authority', *Work, Employment and Society* 8, 1994, pp. 177–198.

Linquist, S. *A History of Bombing*, London: Granta Books, 2001.

Lorentzen, L. A. and J. Turpin (eds) *The Women and War Reader*, New York: New York University Press, 1998.

Lukowiak, K. *Marijuana Time: Join the Army, See the World, Meet Interesting People and Smoke All Their Dope*, London: Orion, 2000, p. 9.

MacDonald, K. 'Black mafia, loggies and going for the stars: the military elite revisted', *Sociological Review* 52 (1), 2004, pp. 106–135.

Macdonald, M. *Exploring Media Discourse*, London: Arnold, 2003.

McNeill, W. H. *Keeping Together in Time: Dance and Drill in Human History*, Cambridge, MA: Harvard University Press, 1995.

Magor, M. 'News terrorism: misogyny exposed and the easy journalism of conflict', *Feminist Media Studies* 12 (1), 2002, pp. 141–144.

Mann, M. *The Sources of Social Power*, Cambridge University Press, Cambridge, 1986.

Manning, L. and V. R. Wright, *Women in the Military: Where they Stand*, 4th edn, Washington DC: Women's Research and Education Institute, 2002.

Mazurana, D. E., A. Raven-Roberts and J. L. Parpart, *Gender, Conflict, and Peacekeeping*, Lanham, MD: Rowman & Littlefield, 2005.

Miller, L. 'Not just weapons of the weak: gender harassment as a form of protest for Army men', *Social Psychology Quarterly* 60, 1997, pp. 32–51.

Miller, L. M. 'Feminism and the exclusion of Army women from combat', *Gender Issues* 16 (3), 1998, pp. 33–64.

Ministry of Defence, *Defence White Paper* Cm4446, London: The Stationery Office, 1999.

—— *The Armed Forces Overarching Personnel Strategy*, London: Ministry of Defence, 2000.

—— *The Wider Employment of Women in Ground Combat*, internal MoD briefing document (unpublished MoD document, c. 2001).

—— *Women in the Armed Forces*, Public Information factsheet. Available at: http://www.mod.uk/DefenceInternet/FactSheets/WomenInTheArmedForces.htm, accessed 17 August 2006.

—— and Equal Opportunities Commission, *Agreement between the Ministry of Defence and the Equal Opportunities Commission on Preventing and Dealing Effectively with Sexual Harassment in the Armed Forces: Progress Report and Phase Three Action Plan, 2006*, Measure 15, Gender Balance in Training.

Mitchell, B. *Women in the Military: Flirting with Disaster*, Washington, DC: Regnery Publishing, 1999.

Moelker, R. and I. van der Kloet, 'Military families and the Armed Forces: a two-sided affair?', in G. Caforio (ed.), *Handbook of the Sociology of the Military*, New York: Plenum Kluwer, 2003.

Morgan, D. *It Will Make a Man of You: Notes on National Service, Masculinity and Autobiography*, Studies in Sexual Politics, University of Manchester, 1987, pp. 1–90.

Morgan, D. H. J. 'Theater of war: combat, the Military, and masculinities', in H. Brod and M. Kaufman (eds), *Theorising Masculinities*, London: Sage, 1994.

Moser, C. and F. Clark (eds) *Victims, Perpetrators or Actors? Gender, Armed Conflict and Political Violence*, New York: Zed Books, 2001.

Moskos, C., J. A. Williams and D. R. Segal (eds) *The Postmodern Military: Armed Forces After the Cold War*, Oxford: Oxford University Press, 2000.

Muir, K. *Arms and the Woman*, London: Coronet, 1993.

Murphy, A. *Is it 'Trouble and Strive' for the British Army Wife? A Study of their Thoughts and Opinions Regarding Identity and Current Access to Support Offered by the Ministry of Defence*, unpublished MA dissertation, School of Geography Politics and Sociology, Newcastle University.

Murphy, L. *Perverts by Official Order: The Campaign Against Homosexuals in the United States Navy*, New York: Harrington Park Press, 1988.

Myers, S. L. 'Why diversity is a smokescreen for affirmative action', *Change*, 29, July/August 1997, pp. 24–32.

Nantais, C. and M. Lee, 'Women in the US Military: Protectors or protected? The case of prisoner of war Melissa Rathbun-Nealy', *Journal of Gender Studies* 8 (2), 1999, pp. 181–191.

NATO (2006) *Committee on Women in the NATO Forces, Country Reports.* Available at: http://www.nato.int/issues/women_nato/index.html, accessed 30 October 2006.

Nixon, S. *Hard Looks: Masculinities, Spectatorship and Contemporary Consumption*, London: UCL Press, 1996.

—— 'Exhibiting masculinity', in S. Hall (ed.), *Representation: Cultural Representations and Signifying Practices*, London: Sage, 1997.

Noakes, L. *Women in the British Army: War and the Gentle Sex, 1907–1948*, London: Routledge, 2006.

Ó Tuathail, G. *Critical Geopolitics: The Politics of Writing Global Space*, London: Routledge, 1997.

—— and S. Dalby (eds) *Rethinking Geopolitics*, London: Routledge, 1998.

Oddy, D. J. 'Gone for a soldier: the anatomy of a nineteenth-century army family', *Journal of Family History* 25 (1), 2000, pp. 39–62.

Osman, M. R. 'Fatherhood impacts on decision-making in conflict', *Defence Studies* 3, 2003, pp. 63–86.

Page, L. *Lions, Donkeys and Dinosaurs: Waste and Blundering in the Armed Forces*, London: Heineman, 2006.

Paris, M. *Warrior Nation: Images of War in British Popular Culture 1850–2000*, London: Reaktion Books, 2000.

Paxman, J. *Friends in High Places: Who Runs Britain?*, Harmondsworth: Penguin, 1991.

Pennington, R. and R. Higham, *Amazons to Fighter Pilots: A Biographical Dictionary of Military Women*, Westport, CT: Greenwood Press, 2003;

Pfarr, D. *Women in the Austrian Armed Forces*, Minerva: Quarterly Report on Women and the Military, Fall/Winter 1999.

Porter, B. D. *War and the Rise of the State*, New York: Free Press, 1994.

Ridge, M. 'UK Military manpower and substitutability', *Defence Economics* 2, 1991, pp. 283–293.

Robbins, J. and U. Ben-Eliezer, 'New roles or 'New Times'? Gender inequality and militarism in Israel's Nation-in-Arms', *Social Politics* 7 (3), 2000, pp. 309–342.

Robinson, J. *Mary Seacole*, London: Constable and Robinson, 2006.

Rosen L. and L. Martin, 'Sexual harassment, cohesion and combat readiness in US Army support units', *Armed Forces & Society* 24, 1997, pp. 221–244.

Roy, T. *Women in Khaki: The Story of the British Woman Soldier*, London: Columbus, 1988.

Royle, T. *The Best Years of their Lives: The National Service Experience, 1945–1963*, London: Michael Joseph, 1986.

Ruger, W., S. Wilson and S. Waddoups, 'Welfare and warfare: military service, combat and marital dissolution', *Armed Forces & Society* 29, 2002, pp. 86–107.

Rutherford, S., R. Schneider and A.Walmsley, *Ministry of Defence/Equal Opportunities Commission Agreement on Preventing and Dealing Effectively with Sexual Harassment: Quantitative and Qualitative Research into Sexual Harassment in the Armed Forces*, London: Schneider Ross, 2006.

Sasson-Levy, O. 'Constructing identities at the margins: masculinities and citizenship in the Israeli army', *Sociological Quarterly* 43, 2002, pp. 353–383.

—— 'Feminism and military gender practices: Israeli women soldiers in "masculine" roles', *Sociological Inquiry*, 73 (3), 2003, pp. 440–465.

—— 'Military, masculinity and citizenship: Tensions and contradictions in the experience of blue-collar soldiers', *Identities': Global Studies in Culture and Power* 10, 2003, pp. 319–345.

Schmitz, C. ' "We too were soldiers": the experiences of British nurses in the Anglo-Boer War, 1899–1902', in G. J. DeGroot and C. Peniston-Bird (eds), *A Soldier and a Woman: Sexual Integration in the Military*, Harlow: Longman, 2000, pp. 49–62.

Segal, M. W. 'The military and the family as greedy institutions', *Armed Forces & Society* 13, 1986, pp. 9–38.

—— 'Women's military roles cross-nationally: past, present and future', *Armed Forces and Society* 9 (6), 1995, pp. 757–775.

Shilts, R. *Conduct Unbecoming: Gays and Lesbians in the US Military*, New York: St. Martin's Press, 1993.

Siegel, M. ' "To the Unknown Mother of the Unknown Soldier": pacifism, feminism and the politics of sexual difference among French *Institutrices* between the wars', *French Historical Studies* 22 (3), 1999, pp. 421–451.

Sion, L. ' "Too Sweet and Innocent for War"? Dutch peacekeepers and the use of violence', *Armed Forces & Society* 32 (3), 2006, pp. 454–474.

Smith, R. *The Utility of Force: The Art of War in the Modern World*, Harmondsworth: Penguin, 2006.

Spurling, K. 'From exclusion to submarines: the integration of Australian women naval volunteers', *Australian Defence Force Journal* 139 (November/December), 1999, pp. 34–40.

Storey, J. *An Introduction to Cultural Theory and Popular Culture*, 2nd edn, Hemel Hempstead: Harvester Wheatsheaf, 1993.

Summerfield, P. and C. Peniston-Bird, 'Women in the firing line: the Home Guard and the defence of gender boundaries in Britain in the Second World War', *Women's History Review* 9, 2000, pp. 231–255.

Tasker, Y. ' "Soldiers" stories: women and military masculinities in *Courage Under Fire*', *Quarterly Review of Film & Video*, 19, 2002, pp. 209–222.

Tatchell, P. *We Don't Want to March Straight*, London: Cassell, 1995.

Thorne, T. *Brasso, Blanco and Bull*, London: Constable and Robinson, 2000.

Thussu, D. K. and D. Freedman, *War and the Media: Reporting Conflict 24/7*, London: Sage, 2003.

Titunik, R. 'The first wave: gender, integration and military culture', *Armed Forces & Society* 26 (2), 2000, pp. 229–257.

Vellacott, J. 'A place for pacifism and transnationalism in feminist theory: the early work of the Women's International League for Peace and Freedom', *Women's History Review* 2 (1), 1993, pp. 23–56.

Vernon, A. (ed.) *Arms and the Self: War, the Military and Autobiographical Writing*, Kent, OH: Kent State University Press, 2005.

Weedon, C. *Feminist Practice and Poststructuralist Theory*, Oxford: Blackwell, 1987.

Weeks, J. *Sexuality and its Discontents*, London: Routledge, 1985.

Wertsch, M. *Military Brats: Legacies of Childhood Inside the Fortress*, New York: Harmony Books, 1991.

Wheelwright, J. *Amazons and Military Maids: Women who Dressed as Men in the Pursuit of Life, Liberty and Happiness*, London: Pandora Press, 1989.

Whitworth, S. *Men, Militarism and UN Peacekeeping: A Gendered Analysis*, Boulder, CO: Lynne Rienner, 2004.

Winslow D. and J. Dunn, 'Women in the Canadian Forces: between legal and social integration', *Current Sociology* 50, 2002, 641–667.

Winter, J. and A. Prost, *The Great War in History: Debates and Controversies, 1914 to the Present*, Cambridge: Cambridge University Press, 2005.

Wojach, A. N. 'Women can be integrated into ground combat units', in J. Haley (ed.), *Women in the Military*, San Diego, CA: Greenhaven, 2002, pp. 27–38.

Woodward, K. 'Motherhood: identities, meanings and myths', in K. Woodward (ed.), *Identity and Difference*, London: Sage, 1997.

Woodward, R. ' "It's a man's life!": soldiers, masculinity and the countryside', *Gender, Place and Culture* 5 (3), 1998, pp. 277–300.

—— 'Warrior heroes and little green men: soldiers, military training, and the construction of rural masculinities', *Rural Sociology* 64 (4), 2000, pp. 640–657.

—— 'Locating military masculinities: space, place, and the formation of gender identity and the British Army', in P. Higate, *Military Masculinities: Identity and the State*, Westport, CT: Praeger, 2003, pp. 43–55.

—— *Military Geographies*, Oxford: Blackwell, 2004.

—— 'From military geographies to militarism's geographies: disciplinary engagements with the geographies of militarism and military activities', *Progress in Human Geography* 29 (6), 2005, pp. 718–740.

—— 'Not for Queen and country or any of that shit . . .: reflections on citizenship and military participation in contemporary British soldier narratives', in E. Gilbert and D. Cowan, *War, Citizenship, Territory*, London: Routledge, 2007 (in press).

—— and P. Winter, 'Discourses of gender in the contemporary British Army', *Armed Forces & Society* 30, 2004, pp. 279–301.

—— and P. Winter, 'Gender and the limits to diversity in the contemporary British Army', *Gender, Work and Organization* 13, 2006, pp. 45–67.

Woolf, V. *Three Guineas*, Harmondsworth: Penguin, 1997 [1938].

von Zugbach, R. and M. Ishaq, *Public Schools and Officer Recruitment in the British Army of the Late 20th Century*, University of Paisley, Working Paper, 1999.

Websites

http://en.wikipedia.org/wiki/Ultimate_Force (accessed 27 October 2006)

http://news.bbc.co.uk/1/hi/scotland/2017213.stm (accessed 31 May 2002)

http://news.bbc.co.uk/1/hi/uk/4554083.stm (accessed 9 December 2006)

http://shared.armyjobs.mod.uk/JobDescriptions/RegularArmy/Combat/Infantry/InfantrySoldier.htm (accessed 9 December 2006)

http://shared.armyjobs.mod.uk/JobDescriptions/RegularArmy/Specialist/Musician.htm (accessed 9 December 2006)

http://www.army.mod.uk/atr/atr_winchester/training/index.htm (accessed 9 December 2006)

http://www.army.mod.uk/atr/atr_winchester/training/index.htm (accessed 9 December 2006)

http://www.armyjobs.mod.uk (accessed 9 December 2006)

http://www.armyjobs.mod.uk/RegularArmy/RolesAndCareers/ (accessed 9 December 2006)

http://www.armyjobs.mod.uk/RegularArmy/RolesAndCareers/ (accessed 9 December 2006)

http://www.imdb.com/title/tt0106138/ (accessed 17 October 2006)

http://www.imdb.com/title/tt0106138/usercomments (accessed 16 October 2006)

http://www.shinycapstar.com/pacesticking05.htm (accessed 9 December 2006)

http://www.ssrc.org/programs/gsc/gsc_quarterly/newsletter5/content/brown.page (accessed 9 December 2006)

http://www.thesun.co.uk/article/0,,2-2005570450,00.html (accessed 30 June 2006)

http://www.youtube.com/watch?v=jjhxekdZl7k (accessed 9 December 2006)

www.bbc.co.uk (accessed 8 November 2005)

Newspapers

News of the World, 11 February 2001.

The Daily Telegraph, 3 April 2001.

The Sun, 6 April 2001.

The Sun, 26 April 2001.

Television

Soldiers to Be, Series 1, Episode 1, 'A New Life', broadcast on BBC Television, 3 August 1999.

Index